House Warming

with Charlie Wing

Also by Charles Wing
    From the Ground Up (WITH JOHN N. COLE)
    From the Walls In
    The Tighter House

House Warming

with Charlie Wing

Drawings by Mary McCarthy

An Atlantic Monthly Press Book

LITTLE, BROWN AND COMPANY · BOSTON · TORONTO

FIRST EDITION

LIBRARY OF CONGRESS CATALOGING IN PUBLICATION DATA

Wing, Charles, 1939-
  House warming.

  "An Atlantic Monthly Press book."
  Includes index.
  1. Dwellings—Heating and ventilation. 2. Dwellings
—Insulation. I. Title.
TH7222.W56 1983   697   83-13623
ISBN 0-316-94668-0

ATLANTIC–LITTLE, BROWN BOOKS
ARE PUBLISHED BY
LITTLE, BROWN AND COMPANY
IN ASSOCIATION WITH
THE ATLANTIC MONTHLY PRESS

Published simultaneously in Canada
by Little, Brown & Company (Canada) Limited

PRINTED IN THE UNITED STATES OF AMERICA

The fortunate person is formed by a succession of forces: mother, father, teacher, and mentor. My fortune extends to the privilege of associating with William Richardson.

Thanks to Mary McCarthy for inspired illustration, Susan Black Wing for handwriting interpretation, Laura Sawyer for gremlin trapping, and Parker Poole III for holding faith.

Contents

1. INTRODUCTION   3
2. HOW HOUSES WORK   15
3. HEATING   28
4. OIL AND GAS FURNACES AND BOILERS   48
5. HEAT FROM THE SUN   63
6. DOORS   79
7. WINDOWS   91
8. COOLING   113
9. THE GENERAL THEORY OF INSULATION   130
10. THE SPECIFIC THEORY OF INSULATION   146
11. HIDDEN HEAT LEAKS   163
12. HOT WATER   171
13. HOUSE WARMING   188
     INDEX   199

House Warming

with Charlie Wing

1. Introduction

Energy is the key to human existence. The three basic human needs—*food*, *clothing*, and *shelter*—are but different facets of energy. Food is the fuel we ingest and internally combust to power our bodies. Clothing, beyond its sexual subleties, is either a form of insulation against winter heat loss, or a form of bodily shading against summer heat gain. Shelter performs the same functions as clothing, but on a much larger scale.

Considering its importance, Americans are remarkably blasé about their use of energy. There are roughly 80,000,000 homes in America, and the amount of energy consumed in them (for the most part wasted) is staggering—the equivalent of 100,000,000,000 gallons of gasoline per year.

Americans consume sixty-five times as much energy per capita as their counterparts in India; nine times as much as the Mexicans; even three and one-half times as much as the Japanese (Illustration 1.1).

Since the Industrial Revolution, America's annual energy consumption has risen rapidly—far more than can be accounted for by population growth alone (Illustration 1.2). After the Arab oil embargo of 1973, because of radical increases in the prices of all energy sources and an impulsive (so it seems now) attempt by the government to educate the public, energy consumption slowed. But it didn't stop, and with the deemphasis on energy conservation by the Reagan Administration, it promises to curve upward again.

THE SITUATION

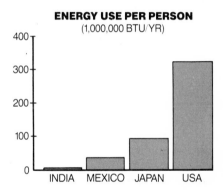

ENERGY USE PER PERSON
(1,000,000 BTU/YR)

1.1

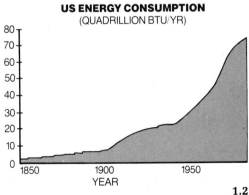

US ENERGY CONSUMPTION
(QUADRILLION BTU/YR)

1.2

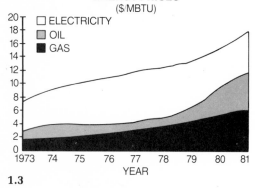

ENERGY PRICES
($/MBTU)

☐ ELECTRICITY
▨ OIL
■ GAS

1.3

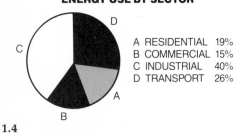

ENERGY USE BY SECTOR

A RESIDENTIAL 19%
B COMMERCIAL 15%
C INDUSTRIAL 40%
D TRANSPORT 26%

1.4

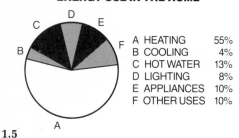

ENERGY USE IN THE HOME

A HEATING 55%
B COOLING 4%
C HOT WATER 13%
D LIGHTING 8%
E APPLIANCES 10%
F OTHER USES 10%

1.5

For many decades as more and more nonrenewable energy sources were discovered and the efficiencies of energy conversion increased, energy prices rose at a slower rate than general inflation. Energy was thus perceived as a relative bargain. The embargo of 1973 marked a turning point, however.

In that year the oil-exporting countries, led by the Arab nations, demonstrated for all future students of economics the validity of the law of supply and demand. They acted on the realization that their greatest natural resource was truly *nonrenewable* and that oil represented a one-time shot at economic development financed by the oil-importing countries. Illustration 1.3 shows what has happened to the prices of No. 2 fuel oil, natural gas, and electricity since supply and demand have taken over. In theory—and in fact—all fuel prices have risen faster than inflation *and probably will as long as the sources are nonrenewable.*

Of the total American energy pie (Illustration 1.4) nearly 20 percent is consumed in the home, and much of the 26 percent in the transportation sector is consumed by the four-wheeled machines in our driveways.

Illustration 1.5 shows that within the average American home, more than half of the energy consumed does no useful work at all, being used merely to heat and/or cool the volume of interior air. An additional 13 percent dribbles down the drain as hot water.

THE POSSIBILITIES

Most of us can remember when Detroit automakers (those wellsprings of American ingenuity) claimed the thirty-mile-per-gallon automobile to be impractical. Today you can drive out of the showroom in models—some of them American—that deliver nearly twice that figure!

I'm going to show you how to do the same thing with your home. In these pages, I'll show you how to save *up to 75 percent of the energy you now pay for* (Illustration 1.6): the first 25 percent, merely by cleaning up your slothful ways; the second 25 percent, through a modest investment in insulation and tightening; and a third 25 percent, if you care to go that far, through a more substantial and longer-range investment in solar energy. The figures in the illustration are nominal; I'll actually achieve these savings for somewhat lower cost, but I don't want to be accused of being overzealous.

THE METHOD

The way I intend to demonstrate these savings is by retrofitting a house. I'm going to *remodel* an older house into an attractive and more livable space but, at the same time, *retrofit* its energy-consuming systems and components into a fuel-efficient machine for the future.

Information on energy conservation is not in short supply. In fact, there may be too much. In every newspaper and magazine we are told to install this gizmo and that. In a single edition of a Sunday newspaper one can find guidance that, if followed, promises to save ten times the total energy we presently consume!

Unfortunately there is no universal best set of solutions. Every home, every homeowner, is unique and requires a unique combination of retrofit actions (yes, the homeowner needs retrofitting as well) in order to produce maximum savings for minimum cost in a comfortable and pleasing environment.

In the words of a teacher I now recognize as having had a disproportionate effect on my character, "I am very pleased to inform you that you will be required to participate." For every energy-consuming aspect of a house — for example, windows — we'll be asking these four questions:

1. What do we expect this thing to do for us?
2. How does it work?
3. What are all of our options for improving this thing?
4. Considering price and performance — and personal taste — what is the best solution?

Of course the answer to the last question will be unique to you and your house. We'll always find the best solutions for *my*

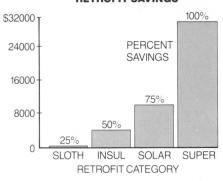

TYPICAL COSTS TO ACHIEVE RETROFIT SAVINGS

1.6

house, but following the same decision-making process will lead you to your own best solutions. Finally, I'll show you, step by step, how to make, repair, or install many of the solutions.

THE HOUSE

The subject of this investigation is my real-life house. My wife, Susan, and I fell in love with the house in passing by several times each day on the way to work or shopping. In twenty years we've lived in eight different houses and three summer cottages. One would think we couldn't make up our minds! But this house was different; it had character and exuded "houseness" — at least New England farmhouseness. The earliest photograph of the house on file at the local historical society is dated 1908 and shows it to be one of two houses in a neighborhood that now contains two score. In 1908 it was surrounded by twenty acres of field; now it is engulfed by suburbia. Yet it retains that essence of farmhouse.

Apparently the former owner, now deceased, possessed the same strength of character. Several of our new neighbors showed a strong interest in us, and in our intentions regarding the house. For a while it looked as if *any* change, inside or out, would be regarded as equivalent to putting vinyl siding on Abraham Lincoln's log cabin.

But I'm not afraid of the old man's ghost. Considering his airlock entry, bricked-up basement sill, and rock-wool insulation installed in the 1940s, I'm sure he would approve of our retrofit.

The building consists of a story-and-a-half main section and a story-and-a-half ell in a style best described as "Carpenter Gothic" — the common man's version of Gothic Revival. It was obviously constructed without benefit of an architect and at minimal cost. What the building lacks in expensive materials and excessive detail, however, it more than makes up in livability and sense of proportion.

As is common in turn-of-the century farmhouses, a spacious porch faces the rising sun to the east (Illustration 1.7). No doubt the porch worked perfectly for the farmer, admitting the

warming early morning sun but providing welcome shade for sessions of post-chore rocking on hot summer afternoons. And as an afterthought, probably inspired by midnight trudges through the Maine snow, a woodshed was added to connect the ell to the barn.

The narrow north face contains three windows (the minimum of one for each of three rooms served) and a formal entrance door, undoubtedly used only by the postman and strangers.

1.8

The west side (Illustration 1.8) is the most interesting one from an energy viewpoint. Somewhere along the line, perhaps after an especially successful year, a bay window was added. The nature of the foundation proves that it was an addition. This windowed projection begs to become a "sunspace," but the total absence of shading on the dog-day-afternoon west side raises a warning flag.

The bottom two-thirds of the south wall is occupied by the woodshed, a structure that, remarkably, still stands, or should I say leans, entirely without benefit of foundation or sills. Even if the woodshed were removed, however, the two-story barn 20 feet to the south would still cast a midwinter-day shadow over the bottom half of the south wall. Solar heating was clearly not uppermost in the farmer's mind.

In order to bring the house down to television-screen size, we had a replica constructed in miniature, built to dollhouse scale (one inch equals one foot). The ingenious nature of the model allows viewing of each floor, in both before and after retrofit configurations. Illustration 1.9 shows the first floor before retrofit. It contains a kitchen in the ell, a dining room with the above-mentioned bay, a living room with windows facing south and east, a parlor facing north and east, and a front hall with stairway. With the exception of the kitchen, all of these first-floor rooms are small by modern standards. A possibility we will

1.9

1.10

investigate in the next chapter is the removal of the interior walls and creation of an open plan.

The second floor (Illustration 1.10) contains two good-sized bedrooms with closets in the main section, a tiny leftover space over the front hall, and an overcrowded bathroom. (The remnants of a two-holer in the woodshed explain the present overcrowding in the bathroom.) Over the kitchen in the ell is a third bedroom with a dormer window facing east. A closet and a back stairway down to the kitchen door block visual access to the south wall. Later on we will investigate removal of the closet to gain access to the sun.

The second floor is a half-story and suffers from short walls, sloping ceilings, and poor daylighting. The short floor-level upstairs windows on the west wall provide too much summer heat, ineffective lighting, and no privacy. You'll have to read on to see what we do about that.

A full basement extends under both main house and ell. Thanks to sandy, well-drained soil and a low water table, the basement is dry as dust. To our good fortune, the entire house is dry, with no evidence of dry rot anywhere. We were lucky, since basements usually provide the greatest amount of interior moisture.

We found a sheaf of coal receipts dated 1929 nailed to a basement joist. They tell us how the farmer used to heat his house, at least until the Great Depression. Presently, the house is heated with a very modern and high-quality oil-burning warm-air furnace. If you just can't wait to see whether we'll abandon the oil furnace, peek into Chapter 3. But come back!

AN ENERGY AUDIT

As a first step in the retrofitting process, I invested in an energy audit. By an act of Congress, most large gas and electric utilities are required to offer their customers Class A Energy Audits (performed on site by a trained inspector) at a charge not to exceed fifteen dollars. Considering the time spent by the very knowledgeable auditor (three hours) and the fact that the audit laid out one version of a comprehensive retrofitting plan complete with estimated costs, savings, and years to payback for twenty different projects, that fifteen dollars was the best investment of the whole project.

I did not follow all of the suggestions contained in the audit report — nor did I ever expect to. For every energy-consuming aspect of a house there are usually half a dozen alternative solutions. The solution finally chosen may be different from that recommended by an audit because of the homeowner's or contractor's personal bias or, just as often, because the details of a project are not fully understood until retrofitting is well along. This did not diminish the value of the audit. I got what I wanted: (1) a three-hour opportunity to consult with an energy expert for $5 an hour; and (2) confirmation of my initial ballpark estimates of the total cost and fuel savings of the planned retrofit.

The detailed audit recommendations are, therefore, not important. The overall or summary figures are interesting,

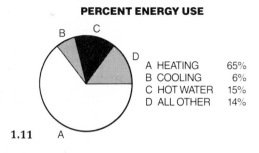

PERCENT ENERGY USE

A	HEATING	65%
B	COOLING	6%
C	HOT WATER	15%
D	ALL OTHER	14%

1.11

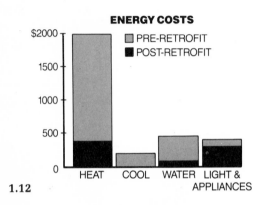

ENERGY COSTS

PRE-RETROFIT
POST-RETROFIT

HEAT   COOL   WATER   LIGHT &
APPLIANCES

1.12

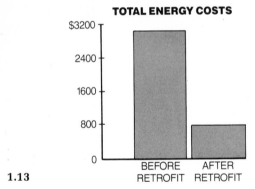

TOTAL ENERGY COSTS

BEFORE RETROFIT   AFTER RETROFIT

1.13

however, in characterizing both the existing house and the savings we might expect to achieve. Illustration 1.11 shows that the pre-retrofit house and occupants consume slightly more energy in both heating and cooling than the national average figure (compare with Illustration 1.5). This reflects the fact that the building is less well insulated than the average because the average includes newer homes as well.

Illustration 1.12 demonstrates the motivation for a thorough retrofit — the savings in energy bills that might accrue: an amazing 80 percent reduction in the cost of heating, total elimination of the cooling bill, and an 82 percent reduction in the cost of heating hot water. Overall, the total annual energy bill (Illustration 1.13) is projected to drop from $3,029 to $776 — a reduction of 75 percent.

The estimated retrofit cost of $9,000 to achieve a 75 percent energy reduction illustrates an important point. The best time to *retrofit* is during *remodeling*. In fact, if you remodel without retrofitting, you'll blow a once-in-a-lifetime opportunity. Houses are extensively remodeled on an average cycle of about forty years. Since the bathrooms, woodshed, and bay window were all added about forty years ago, this house conforms to that cycle and is ready for a second round.

Achieving a 75 percent energy saving in a well-maintained house is likely to be more expensive, since the final cosmetic stages of the work must be billed to retrofit rather than remodeling. In such a case, a 50 percent savings might be a more realistic goal. By subtotaling the audit figures, I found that I could have reduced my annual energy bill by 50 percent for a total investment of $4,000.

THE CONSERVATION INVESTMENT GAME

A surprising number of people display the same attitude about investments as a former neighbor of mine. Most of these people have their money "invested" in savings accounts returning less than the inflation rate. One midwinter day we were talking about our heating bills. As I compared the size of his house to his heating bill, I surmised that his house was totally uninsulated. In response he looked me straight in the eye and announced that he *couldn't afford to insulate his house!*

In case you find yourself in this quandary I'd like to share with you a hot investment tip. You can't, in fact, afford *not* to insulate your house! What's more, you can make money without investing a cent of your own.

I'll use this house as an example. I found that I could reduce the total annual energy bill by 75 percent for $9,000; or, taking a more conservative approach, 50 percent for $4,000. Let's use the 50-percent–$4,000 figures. Before retrofitting, the total energy bill was $3,000, so I could *save* $1,500 per year by *spending* $4,000 once. Let's assume that, like my neighbor, I don't have the $4,000. No problem! Here's how it works.

Illustration 1.14 shows four people sitting around a table. The arrows between the people show the financial transactions the first year.

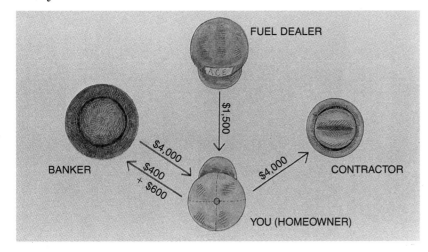

FUEL DEALER

$1,500

BANKER $4,000 $400 + $600 $4,000   CONTRACTOR

YOU (HOMEOWNER)

1.14

STEP 1. I borrow $4,000 from the bank for 10 years at 15 percent interest. To make it simple, I have to repay 1/10 of the loan principal ($400 per year) plus 15 percent interest on the loan ($600 per year) every year for 10 years.

STEP 2. I then pay the contractor(s) $4,000 for the retrofit work, which results in a reduction of my energy bill by $1,500.

STEP 3. Since I am on a monthly fuel payment plan, my fuel supplier rebates the $1,500 I didn't spend this year.

STEP 4. I make the bank payment of $400 principal and $600 interest — leaving me with $500!

For the next nine years I'll continue to receive $1,500 in fuel rebates, and continue to pay $1,000 to the bank. This leaves me every year with $500 I wouldn't otherwise have had.

The table in the illustration demonstrates how it happens. Over the ten-year period the banker, the contractor, and I all benefit at the expense of the fuel dealer. The best part is that I never spend a cent of my own!

Note: In case you're worried about the oversimplification in my figures, the actual annual loan payment would be $774, rather than $1,000, and the end-of-ten-year figures would be:

> Banker = +$3,740
>
> Contractor = +$4,000
>
> Me = +$7,260
>
> Fuel Dealer = −$15,000.

Now, let's get down to work and start making some money! I'm already dreaming of ways to spend my $7,260 windfall.

2. *How Houses Work*

The most common dilemma facing homeowners who want to save energy is knowing where to start. Unfortunately, the King of Hearts' advice to "begin at the beginning" is poor counsel. In retrofitting, the order in which one proceeds *does* make a difference. Energy-saving measures often promise the impossible result of saving the same energy twice.

The first step in my retrofit was the energy audit, which contained energy-saving recommendations listed in an order that would result in the greatest savings for the least cost.

How do energy auditors know which actions to recommend? They know because they understand *how houses work*. And that, dear reader, is what this chapter is about.

FUNCTIONS OF THE HOUSE

First of all, what *is* a house? Webster's dictionary defines a house as anything which serves an animal for shelter or habitation. By that rather all-encompassing definition sea shells, birds' nests, castles, and Winnebagos are all houses. But I've always thought that things are best defined indirectly by the functions expected of them.

The functions we expect of a house are numerous, often taken for granted, and sometimes funny. A partial list includes:

2.1

• **Keeping us warm in winter** (Illustration 2.1). Warmth is not a line etched on a thermometer; it is a sensation of cozy comfort—and in winter, the cozier the better! Two houses maintained at identical temperatures can be quite different in level of comfort.

2.2

• **Keeping us cool in summer** (Illustration 2.2). When summer rolls around, we expect the same house that provided warmth in winter to furnish "coolth." Again, the sensation of comfort is more important than temperature alone and, as we will see in Chapter 8, is a rather complex function.

• **Keeping us dry** (Illustration 2.3). Man may trace his ancestry to the sea, but there is no question that the modern version of the species is more comfortable dry than wet. And many of our prized furnishings fare worse than we when subjected to moisture. A roof is to a house as an umbrella is to a person, so a house should provide ample overhangs.

2.4

• **Holding up a snow load** (Illustration 2.4). Among the weights that a building roof is called upon to bear are: itself, snow, snow saturated with rain, falling limbs, birds, and people.

2.5

- **Supporting occupants and furnishings** (Illustration 2.5). Floors are usually designed to hold up to 40 pounds per square foot. Public buildings are required by law to support 100 pounds per square foot. Some houses are more public than others.

2.6

- **Withstanding wind and earthquake** (Illustration 2.6). Houses should be designed to survive the worst Nature serves up. Some old houses are still around; a surprising number are not, although more succumb to fire and bulldozer than to the forces of Nature.

The list could be longer, but it illustrates the diverse demands we place on a house. The apparent diversity is, however, deceptive. Actually, all of these functions fall into one of two categories:

1. Resisting a physical force
2. Resisting a flow of heat.

These are quite different functions. It should not surprise us that the house performs them using two different sets of principles. Let's examine the functions one at a time.

A wide variety of forces act within and upon a house. First, there is the weight of the house itself. You may have noticed that carpenters tend to be rugged types. That's because houses weigh between 30,000 and 50,000 pounds, not including their foundations. Then, there are the less constant but sometimes considerable weights of occupants, friends, and furnishings. A well-attended party, such as often occurs when the parents of a teenager leave town, may add a transient 10,000 pounds! In cold northern climates the weight of snow on the roof may at times equal or exceed the weight of the house itself. And finally, there are the rare but potentially more destructive dynamic forces of wind and earthquake.

Houses are made of brick, stone, and even mud; but houses are most often made of wood. Wood is Nature's most amazing material, being pound for pound stronger than all but the strongest steels. Unlike steel, however, it is fairly unpredictable and requires the application of a large design safety factor. The strength lies in its stringy fibers and so varies markedly with the way the wood is cut. In the direction of the fibers (grain of the wood) it is very strong, but across the grain it is very weak. A 3/4″-thick board is so weak cross-grain that even I have no trouble amazing my friends on occasion with a swift, board-splitting karate chop.

A piece of wood lying on its face (Illustration 2.7) is called either a "board" or a "plank," depending on its thickness. In either case, it is very springy. The same piece of wood turned on

RESISTING PHYSICAL FORCES

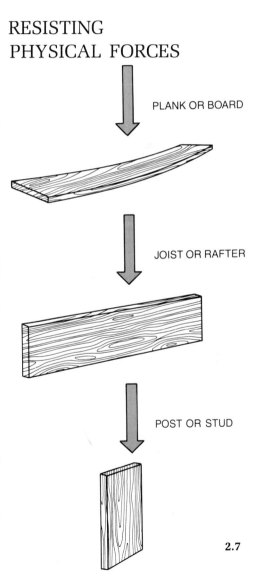

PLANK OR BOARD

JOIST OR RAFTER

POST OR STUD

2.7

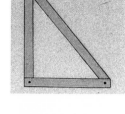

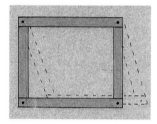

2.8

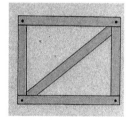

edge is given the name floor "joist" or roof "rafter" and is capable of carrying far greater loads with smaller deflection. The greatest load of all can be carried when the wood is turned on end and used as a wall "stud" or "post."

A house is built with thousands of pieces of wood, and individual wood members may be nailed together in any number of geometric patterns. But a rather remarkable fact is that, of all possible geometric figures, only the triangle is rigid. Illustration 2.8 shows that, while a square or rectangle is easily distorted into a parallelogram by a sideways thrust, the same is not true of a triangle. Altering the shape of a triangle requires changing the length of one or more of the sides of the triangle, and since wood is strongest in the direction of its grain or length, it resists. Note in Illustration 2.8 that a rectangle is quickly altered to two triangles by the simple addition of a diagonal "brace."

The wood components of a house that resist physical forces are these same boards, planks, joists, rafters, studs, posts, and triangular braces. All together we call the assemblage of pieces the house frame. Illustration 2.9 shows a typical "balloon frame," of which our house is an example. The balloon frame is identified by its 2" × 4" wall studs extending unbroken from foundation to roof.

The rafters at the top support the weight of the roof itself plus the weight of any accumulated ice and snow. This load is transferred downward from the outer ends of the rafters to the wall studs. Similarly, floor joists support the weight of the floor itself plus the building's occupants and furnishings. The load of the floor joists is transferred at the ends of the joists to the wall studs. The downward thrust of the studs and posts (studs at the building corners) is collected by the sill—that horizontal, bottommost piece of wood which marries the building to its foundation. Finally, the foundation transfers the entire building load to the earth, somewhere below that zone of seasonal instability—the frost line.

You can see that a house frame consists of many rectangles and, as such, is prey to the horizontal thrusts of wind and

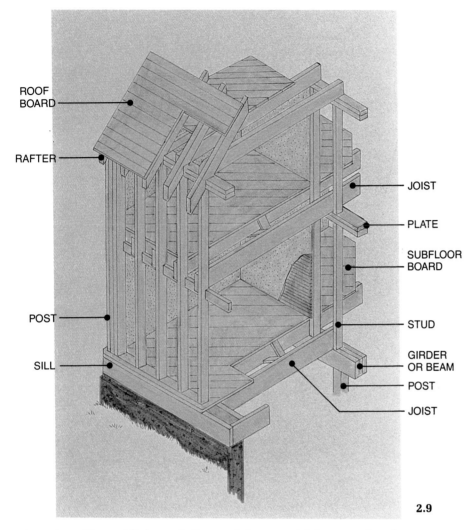

ROOF BOARD

RAFTER

POST

SILL

JOIST

PLATE

SUBFLOOR BOARD

STUD

GIRDER OR BEAM

POST

JOIST

2.9

earthquake. The addition of diagonal braces (either as clearly identifiable members or as an infinite number of braces hidden within a plywood membrane) magically transforms the building frame into a rigid entity.

The span or width of a building often exceeds the ability of a floor joist to carry its load. Introducing an interior wall or post effectively breaks the load into two smaller spans. A wall serving this purpose is a "bearing wall"; in other words, it bears the weight of the floor joists above it.

Most members of the frame serve some load-bearing function. If we understand the function of each member of the frame, then we can alter the frame — as long as we ensure that the required load-bearing functions are satisfied. And if we can alter the frame, it follows that we can alter the interior spaces, because the frame defines the spaces.

Altering Interior Spaces

You will recall from Illustration 1.9 that the first floor of our house contained three rooms which were rather small and redundant in use by modern standards: a dining room with bay window, a living room, and a front parlor. Removing the walls between these rooms would result in three improvements: better daylighting, more even heat distribution, and a more dramatic, open plan.

The walls to be removed include one oriented north to south and a second wall running east to west. Before donning hard hat and dust mask and revving up the chain saw, we should pause to remember that interior walls are sometimes load-bearing. Do either of these walls perform a function beyond defining spaces? Will the ceiling above come crashing down?

Identifying bearing walls is detective work. Our first clue is in the basement. There we find a large wood beam measuring $6'' \times 10''$ in cross-section running under the floor joists in a north-south direction. With the help of a tape measure we determine that this beam lies exactly under the north-south wall we are considering eliminating. (Electric cables entering the floor directly above the beam provide another clue.) Obviously, the first-floor joists are not sufficiently strong over their full span to carry the weight of the first floor plus the weight of the north-south wall, and the beam is used to break up the span.

A second clue is found on the second floor. There we find another north-south wall lying directly on top of the first-floor wall. Brace yourself for the following brilliant deduction: the first-floor wall must be doing for the second floor what the basement beam is doing for the first floor — *supporting* it. Therefore the first-floor wall is a bearing wall and we cannot remove it without first providing a structural replacement.

What sort of replacement? A further deduction: what serves

to support the first floor should support the essentially identical second floor — a beam. Illustration 2.10 shows how we replaced the load-bearing wall with a beam.

STEP 1. Construct a temporary stud wall 1/2″ less in height (for clearance) than the floor-to-ceiling height of the wall to be replaced. This stud wall is most easily constructed on the floor and then raised into place.

STEP 2. Raise the stud wall into place about 2 feet away from the existing wall (to allow working space when removing the old wall). Shim under the stud wall with shingles so that the ceiling will not drop when the old wall is removed. NOTE: Make sure at this point that the ceiling joists above are either continuous or amply overlapped and nailed together so that the temporary wall will hold up the *entire* ceiling. If not, you'll have to construct a second temporary wall.

STEP 3. Remove the old wall. You'll find it much easier and neater to remove one type of material at a time, i.e., all the plaster, then all the lath, then the studs. Wetting the

Replacing a Wall With a Beam

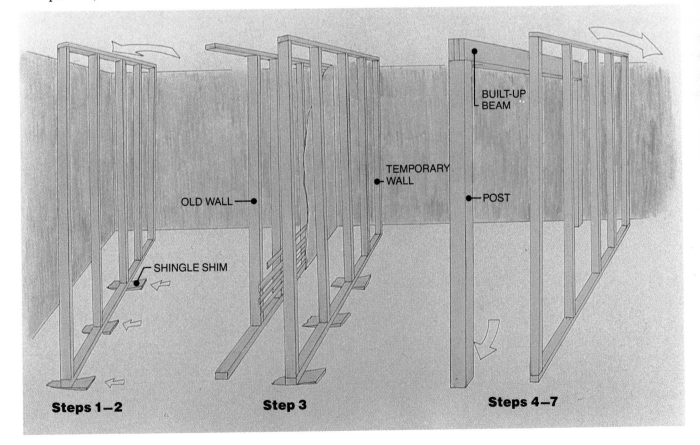

OLD WALL

SHINGLE SHIM

TEMPORARY WALL

BUILT-UP BEAM

POST

Steps 1—2   **Step 3**   **Steps 4—7**

plaster thoroughly several hours before removal will dramatically reduce the amount of dust produced. And don't throw away that lath! You'll find numerous applications later in filling and shimming, and what's left can't be beat as kindling for fires.

STEP 4. Fabricate a beam sufficient to span the length of wall removed. If in doubt as to the required cross-section and span, use the basement beam as a guide. Remember — what holds up the first floor should hold up the second. And if your town has a building inspector, check to see that he agrees with your analysis. Two heads are better than none.

STEP 5. Lay the beam on the floor in the location of the old wall. At each end of the beam hold a post up against the ceiling and mark the location of the top surface of the beam against the post bottom. The post should be just the right length if cut along this line.

STEP 6. You'll need some helpers with this one. Hold the beam in place against the ceiling, the tops of the end posts against the beam, and drive the post bottoms home with a sledgehammer. Shim any slack by driving shingles under the post bottoms. NOTE: There should be either a beam or post in the basement directly beneath each post placed upstairs. If not, add one.

STEP 7. Carefully and slowly remove the temporary stud wall. Removing the shimming shingles first will indicate whether you have succeeded and at the same time leave a safety backup. Success is indicated by the temporary wall carrying no load. For a more thorough treatment of structure, including procedures and tables for posts, joists, rafters, and beams, refer to Chapters 3, 4, and 5 of *From the Walls In*.

RESISTING A FLOW OF HEAT

Now let's consider that second category of house functions — resisting or retarding heat flow either into or out of the house. In the winter we wish to slow the escape of expensive fuel-produced heat to the cold outside; in the summer, we hope to retard the flow of broiling outdoor heat into our cool domicile.

Humans have a difficult time visualizing heat flow. That's because heat is invisible to the human eye. If heat were instead a bright red fluid (which evolution has conditioned our eyes to regard with alarm), there wouldn't be an energy crisis at all. Into every place from which we found red fluid oozing we would stuff insulation or caulk!

To help conceptualize and visualize heat flow into and out of buildings, engineers have invented the "thermal envelope." Heat always flows from warmer to cooler places, whether upward, downward, or sideways. In winter the living space is warmer than the outdoors and so the heat flow is from inside to outside. On a hot summer day the outside is warmer than inside and so the heat flow reverses. The *thermal envelope* is the contiguous collection of building surfaces separating inside space from outside space. Put another way, the thermal envelope is all of those surfaces that are warm on one side and cold on the other.

Illustration 2.11 depicts a simple thermal envelope. If insulation is placed between the rafters in the attic, then the attic

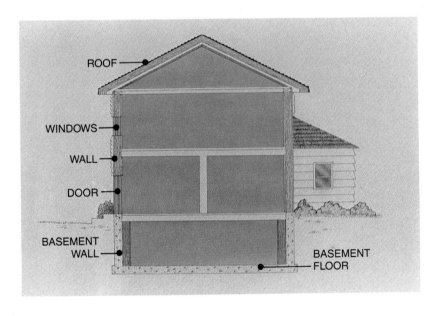

2.11

becomes part of the warm space and the *roof* is then part of the thermal envelope. Obviously the *exterior walls* are part of the thermal envelope. Not so obvious are those special openable sections of wall we call *doors* and *windows*.

Heat, like the residents of Baltimore in the summer, has one desire in life — to escape to a cooler place. Contrary to popular opinion, then, it will flow downward and into the earth if that is a route which ultimately leads outdoors. Therefore basement walls are part of the thermal envelope in a house with a heated basement. Even the basement floor is part of the thermal envelope, although its heat loss is less severe because of the moderate temperatures that prevail in the soil directly below.

Ignoring a single surface of the thermal envelope, no matter how small, is akin to forgetting the drain plug when launching a boat. Sooner or later that bright red fluid will escape.

The Three Roads to Ruin

Heat escapes from the thermal envelope in three different ways (Illustration 2.12). First, since heat is not a substance but a form of energy, it can flow right through an apparently solid

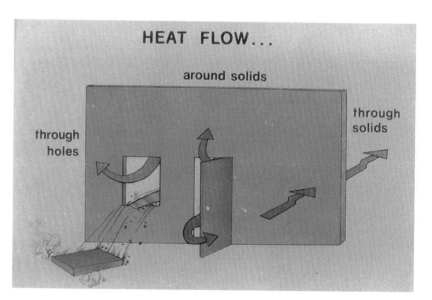

HEAT FLOW...

around solids

through holes

through solids

2.12

surface — rather rapidly, as through metal or glass, or rather slowly, as through a piece of insulating foam. We define the ability of a thermal envelope surface to stop heat flow through it as its "R value." The R value of a single-glazed window is about 1; the R value of a 6″ batt of fiberglass insulation is 19 (it says so right on the package). The fiberglass batt therefore allows $\frac{1}{19}$ as much heat flow as a single-glazed window per square foot of surface.

Heat can also flow around and between the separate surfaces of the thermal envelope. Some of the joints between surfaces are present on purpose; they are designed to be movable joints, such as those around windows and doors. Heat loss here is stopped by weatherstripping. And heat can flow through fixed cracks and defects in and between thermal envelope surfaces. These leaks are stopped by caulking. We call the ability of the overall thermal envelope to stop the exchange of inside and outside air its "airtightness," measured in air exchanges per hour.

In order to improve our thermal envelope, then, we need to take three steps:

STEP 1 (the most difficult by far). Identify all of the surfaces that form our thermal envelope.
STEP 2 (compared with STEP 1, a piece of cake). Increase the R value of each surface through the proper installation of the optimum amount of the appropriate type of insulation.
STEP 3 (time-consuming but inexpensive). Plug all of the joints, cracks, and defects with weatherstripping and caulk.

Before we can determine how much insulation is justified, however, we need to know how much our heat is worth. There's no sense in spending money to save a worthless commodity! So in Chapter 3 we will study our heating alternatives. The heating system and fuel we select will determine the cost-effectiveness of our thermal envelope measures.

3. *Heating*

INTRODUCTION

How far should we go in this energy conservation game? That is, how much money should we spend up front in order to save later fuel dollars? That depends on how much we think we can save. If we use electricity both to heat and to cool our house, energy bills are likely to be large. Possible savings, however, are also likely to be large. On the other hand, if we only heat the house, and do it with wood obtained at the cost of running our chain saw, then there isn't much to save except time and bother. Assuming we are afflicted with the Puritan work ethic and derive perverse pleasure from cutting, hauling, splitting, stacking, and carrying wood, the amount we are willing to invest in conservation may be smaller. So before considering how much to invest in insulation, house tightening, and fuel-displacing solar energy, we should first decide *how to heat our house.*

FUNCTIONS OF THE HEATING SYSTEM

As with every other area of energy use, we must first understand and acknowledge our expectations. Otherwise we will not be in a position to evaluate fully our heating options. A system should:

3.1

● **Provide heat in winter** (Illustration 3.1). Even if one possesses Bean boots, the need at least to temper the cold of a long northern winter seems obvious.

3.2

● **Keep pipes from freezing** (Illustration 3.2). This function never seems to occur to homebuilders until after the dreaded event. Every January night a double-feature plays in my dream theater—the scene shown in the illustration, alternating with a scene starring me on my back in a wet two-foot-high crawl space, holding an underpowered hair dryer to a pipe.

3.3

• **Be clean** (Illustration 3.3). When I was a child it always seemed strange to me that electric, gas, and oil companies stressed "clean heat" in their advertisements. Now that I have a wood stove, I know what they're talking about. I can tell that advertisements depicting a glowing family gathered around a wood stove are fake because there's no trail of dirt and bark leading to the stove and no holes burned in the carpet!

3.4

• **Be safe** (Illustration 3.4). Heating systems are as safe as automobiles. They are safe as long as one realizes that they are potentially dangerous, and operates and maintains them with respect.

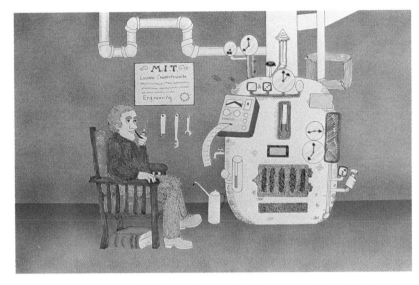

3.5

• **Be convenient** (Illustration 3.5). The operation of a heating system should not require a degree in engineering. Nor should it require knob-twiddling and constant adjustment—unless, of course, your unfulfilled dream is to be a building super.

3.6

• **Provide low-cost heat** (Illustration 3.6). This is the bottom line. The fact that you have stuck with me as far as Chapter 3 indicates an awareness of this function. My apologies to all the fine human beings associated with the oil-heat industry; I just couldn't resist the illustration!

HOW DO HEATING SYSTEMS WORK?

Most heating systems either directly or indirectly involve three separate processes. The first is *combustion*, the conversion of the chemical energy in a fuel to heat energy. The gases produced by combustion — often called stack or flue gases — are not nice. They include carbon dioxide, carbon monoxide, water vapor, sulfur dioxide, and nitrogen dioxide. A more technical term for "not nice" is "pollutant" — any substance added to air or water that alters its natural composition in an undesirable way. Thus carbon dioxide and water vapor, both of which occur naturally in air, are pollutants if added in excessive amounts. A candle on your dinner table gives off the same gases, but we don't consider it a polluter; a furnace is a different matter.

The second process is *conversion* — the transfer of heat from the undesirable flue gases to a safer medium such as air, water, or steam.

Finally, we're interested in heating the entire house, not just the boiler room; and so the third process is *distribution* of the heat to the points of use.

An example of an unsatisfactory heating system is the burning of newspapers in a wastebasket (Illustration 3.7). This

3.7

is unsatisfactory because it ignores Process Two; it doesn't transfer the heat from the flue gases to a safer medium.

A giant step for personkind (at least the kind that lives in my neck of the woods) was taken by Benjamin Franklin when he invented what is essentially the modern woodstove. Illustration 3.8 is not an exact replica of Ben's stove, but it demonstrates the basic concepts. Combustion, or burning of the wood fuel, occurs in a fire chamber. The nasty flue gases escape by way of a stove pipe into a chimney and thence to the outside. Conversion, or transfer of heat from the flue gases to room air, occurs through the cast-iron sides and top of the stove. Distribution of heat to the surrounding room occurs through two mechanisms: (1) the room air warmed through contact with the stove surfaces rises buoyantly, causing a convective circulation of air; and (2) the hot stove surfaces emit infrared or heat radiation in all directions, which then reconverts to heat upon striking surrounding room and people surfaces.

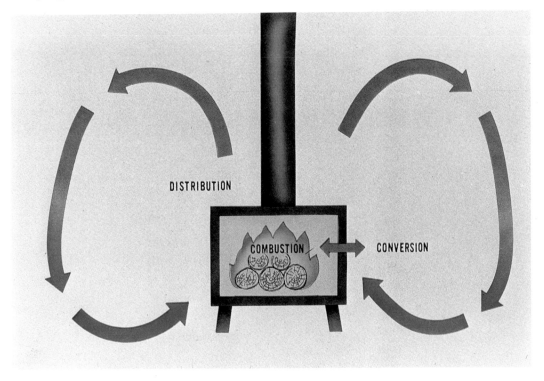

3.8

Even more sophisticated systems include furnaces and boilers. Illustration 3.9 shows the innards of an oil-fired hydronic or hot-water boiler. Let's trace the chain of events triggered by turning up the thermostat.

1. The thermostat turns on the system and a fuel pump sends liquid fuel oil down a tube inside the blast tube of the oil burner. At the end of the blast tube a nozzle sprays or atomizes the oil into very fine droplets, much like a perfume atomizer.

2. At the same time the oil-burner blower (fan) forces air down the blast tube, where it emerges in a turbulent pattern, mixing with the oil droplets to produce a highly combustible state.

3. Simultaneously a high-voltage electric spark jumps across the burner electrodes, igniting the oil-air mixture. The burning mixture fills the combustion chamber with flame.

4. The hot flue gases then flow through a heat exchanger located just above the combustion chamber. After passing through the heat exchanger, the flue gases pass safely through the flue pipe and chimney to the outside.

5. On the other side of the metal walls of the heat exchanger is the safe distribution medium—in this case, either water or steam; in the case of a furnace, air.

6. The warm distribution medium is then pumped or blown through the distribution pipes or ducts to the remote areas of the house. Return pipes or ducts bring the cooled distribution medium back to be heated again and again.

At first glance, electric resistance baseboards appear to be entirely different but, as Illustration 3.10 shows, appearances can be deceiving. Electric resistance or baseboard heating most often involves the same three steps. A fuel is combusted at the electric power plant. The resulting heat generates steam, which drives a turbine by which the heat is converted to electricity. The electricity is distributed to and through the house with wires. Only one further step is required: the electricity is reconverted to heat in the resistance elements of the electric heater.

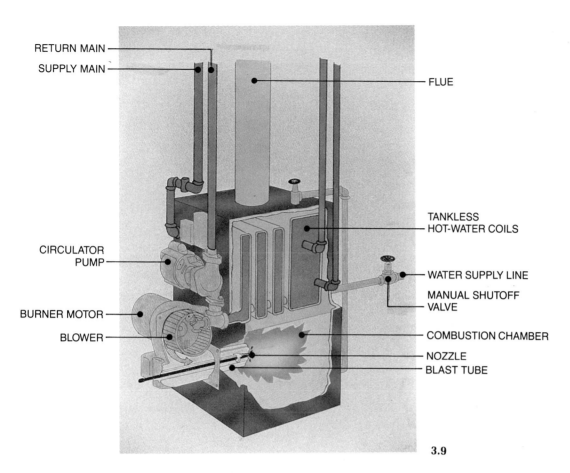

RETURN MAIN

SUPPLY MAIN

FLUE

TANKLESS HOT-WATER COILS

CIRCULATOR PUMP

WATER SUPPLY LINE

MANUAL SHUTOFF VALVE

BURNER MOTOR

BLOWER

COMBUSTION CHAMBER

NOZZLE

BLAST TUBE

3.9

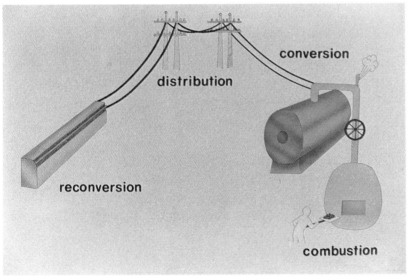

conversion

distribution

reconversion

combustion

3.10

Thus we see that all heating systems are quite similar in physical principle; what makes them different is the cost of the heat they produce.

THE RELATIVE COST OF HEAT

So let us investigate that most interesting function of the heating system — providing low-cost heat. First we have to get our ducks in a row. We are all familiar with the variety of units in which fuels are bought and sold: gallons of oil; therms or CCF (hundreds of cubic feet) of gas; cords of wood; kilowatt-hours of electricity. But comparing fuels on that basis alone is like comparing the value of a grape to the value of a zucchini. What we need is a single unit or measure that allows us to compare all fuels. That unit is the British thermal unit, or Btu: the amount of heat required to raise the temperature of a pound (pint) of water by one Fahrenheit degree.* Raising the temperature of a gallon of water (eight pints) by 10° would require $8 \times 10 = 80$ Btu. Although the following equivalents are not exact, some people find these measures more useful:

Heat from a wood kitchen match = 1 Btu
Heat needed to make one pint
    of tea from cold water   = 100 Btu
Useful heat from one gallon of oil = 100,000 Btu

Unfortunately, pouring a gallon of gasoline into a Volkswagen Rabbit doesn't guarantee that you'll get 50 miles down the turnpike. Similarly, purchasing 100,000 Btu of fuel energy doesn't necessarily mean you'll end up with 100,000 Btu of heat in your house. The Btu content of fuel is defined in terms of what it *can do*, not what it *will do*. The difference lies in the efficiency of the heating system: the efficiency of combustion, efficiency of conversion, and efficiency of distribution.

Efficiency is defined as the ratio of the amount of heat that ends up in the living space (within the thermal envelope) to the amount consumed by the heating system. As such,

$$\text{Efficiency} = \frac{\text{will do}}{\text{can do}}$$

*NOTE: All temperatures throughout this book are given in degrees Fahrenheit.

For example the energy content of one gallon of No. 2 fuel oil is roughly 140,000 Btu. If, during burning, 100,000 Btu of heat are delivered to the living space and 40,000 Btu escape up the chimney and elsewhere, then the efficiency of the heating system is:

$$\text{Efficiency} = \frac{100,000 \text{ Btu}}{140,000 \text{ Btu}} = 71 \text{ percent}$$

A convenient quantity for the bottom-line cost of fuel in heating systems is the *cost per 100,000 Btu delivered heat*. That figure depends on three things: (1) the price paid per unit of fuel; (2) the Btu content per unit of fuel; and (3) the efficiency of the heating system in converting and delivering heat energy from fuel energy. Illustration 3.11 shows the bottom-line costs resulting from combining these three factors for the most common fuels. The notes at the bottom of the illustration list the fuel prices, efficiencies, and energy contents assumed. The fuel prices are intended to be national average figures for the winter of 1982–83. Fortunately, they are also sufficiently close to the prevailing prices in my area to be applicable to my house.

As the heights of the bars show, electric resistance heating at $1.99 per delivered 100,000 Btu is likely to be your most expensive alternative. Installing an electric heat pump can reduce the cost significantly; in my area, down to $1.25. My climate is cold, which leads to a low average efficiency over the heating season. In warmer areas, the efficiency of a heat pump could be significantly higher, resulting in a lower cost of delivered heat. But, if available at reasonable prices in your area, coal and wood are likely to provide the lowest-cost heat.

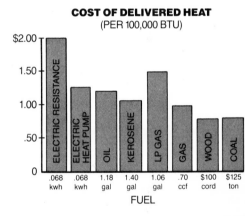

COST OF DELIVERED HEAT
(PER 100,000 BTU)

3.11

THE TRUE COST — LIFE-CYCLE COST

To operate a heating system you first have to purchase the system. Your true cost is the *total* cost of owning and operating a heating system. To the cost of fuel you must add the equipment purchase cost and any other costs, such as maintenance. Economists call this total cost over the useful life of the system the "Life-Cycle Cost" (LCC). Considering taxes, maintenance, inflation, and finance charges, the calculation of LCC can be very complicated and uncertain. Whatever the result, however, it is not likely to be far different from:

$$LCC = \text{equipment cost} + \text{lifetime fuel cost}$$

Illustration 3.12 shows the simple LCC of my alternatives. These numbers assume a twenty-year system life, and a post-retrofit annual heating requirement of 56,500,000 Btu (roughly equivalent to 565 gallons of oil) predicted by my energy audit. The reasonable installation cost of electric resistance heating (ER) does little to ameliorate the high relative cost of using it. The higher efficiency of an electric heat pump (EHP) more than offsets its high initial equipment cost, making it a cheaper alternative than electric resistance even in my cold climate. Both systems, however, promise to be significantly more expensive over a twenty-year period than oil, kerosene, liquefied petroleum (LP) gas, and natural gas. Finally, coal and wood still promise the lowest LCC, primarily because of low fuel cost.

Since I do enjoy splitting and handling a reasonable amount of wood, I've selected a wood stove for my primary heating system.

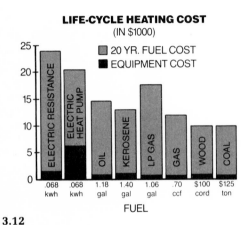

LIFE-CYCLE HEATING COST
(IN $1000)

3.12

WOOD STOVES
How Big?

In selecting a wood stove for a primary heating system, the most important question is, "How big?" If we select a stove that is too small, we'll be unable to maintain a comfortable temperature on the coldest days, or the stove won't burn overnight. On the other hand, a stove that is too large must be burned at a slow rate, resulting in excessive smoke and creosote production.

If we have to select a single stove, the ideal is one that produces heat at the same rate as the average midwinter building heat loss while being fed on a convenient schedule. In my opinion, and for my life-style, such a schedule involves stove-stoking at:

Out of bed (6 A.M.)

Off to work (8 A.M.)

Return from work (6 P.M.)

Into bed (9 P.M.)

Such a schedule translates into: (1) rapid, hot low-smoke burns from 6 A.M. to 10 A.M. and from 6 P.M. to midnight; (2) rekindling at 6 A.M. and 6 P.M.; and (3) a total daily wood consumption of four times the firebox capacity in cubic feet.

From experience in burning wood on this schedule and from conversion factors between the different fuel units, I've developed a rule of thumb for sizing a stove. The rule assumes operating a single wood stove on the schedule shown. If, owing to the layout of your house, you operate two wood stoves simultaneously, the firebox volume in the rule of thumb should be the total of both firebox volumes.

Illustration 3.13 defines the "volume" of the firebox—the volume in cubic feet of that space which you normally fill with

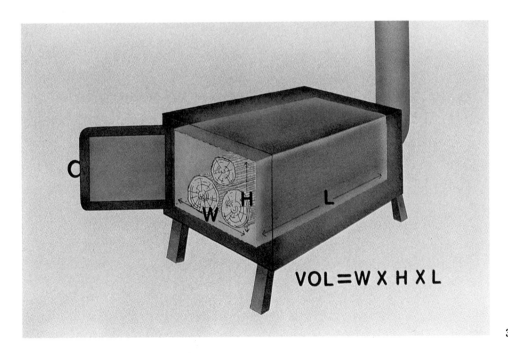

3.13

wood. If, for example, your stove is capable of taking 24″ (2-foot) logs, but you normally burn wood cut to 16″ (1⅓ feet), then the 1⅓ feet should be used instead of the theoretical 2 feet.

My rule of thumb is to install a wood stove (or stoves) containing:

1 cubic foot of firebox for each
- 3 cords of wood
- 360 gallons of oil
- 500 CCF or therms of gas
- 10,000 kwh of electricity

consumed during the entire heating season.

My energy audit predicted that after insulating, caulking, weatherstripping, and everything else, I would burn about 565 gallons of oil. By my rule of thumb, therefore, I need a firebox volume of:

$$565/360 = 1½ \text{ cubic feet}$$

Where to Put the Wood Stove

The second but most subtle and confusing issue in wood heating is where to install the stove. This question confuses and confounds the wood heat novice because it involves weighing and balancing: (1) the possible cost of a new chimney installation; (2) the positive social value of drawing people together; and (3) the need for uniform distribution of heat. If we are both creative and lucky we will find a location that satisfies all three criteria. I believe the solution for my house perfectly illustrates this balancing act.

Chimneys. The present house has two brick chimneys, as can be seen from the illustrations in the first chapter. One is located at the south end of the ell, far from the center of the house. It has been previously retrofitted with a stainless steel pipe and was used by the prior occupants for a kitchen wood stove. The second is centrally located in the main house. It, too, has a stainless steel liner and presently serves the oil furnace. After removal of the first-floor interior walls, it now stands exposed in the center of the new open-plan living space. Either of the chimneys could be used without further modification or cost.

Social Value. Some families congregate in the kitchen; some in the living room; still others, in a family room. Mine apparently descended from the living-room branch, because I most often find them draped over and slouched within living-room couches and chairs. The first two criteria thus point strongly to the living-room chimney hookup. Hopefully, the third criterion will point in the same direction.

Heat Distribution. Obviously, the living-room chimney is more centrally located than the chimney in the ell. Before we conclude that installing a wood stove there will result in an acceptably uniform heating of the entire house, however, we need to understand how warm air flows.

How Warm Air Flows

From childhood we have heard that "warm air rises." Hot-air balloons and smoke from the ends of cigarettes indeed experientially confirm the aphorism. Conversely, we say that "cool air falls." These two statements are all we need in order to understand and predict the marvelous flow of air around a wood stove.

Illustration 3.14A shows that the combination of warm air rising from a hot wood stove and cooled air falling along thermal

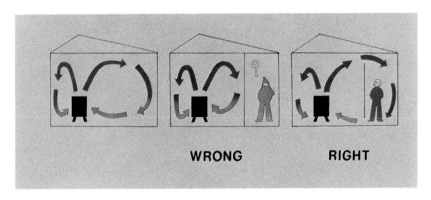

WRONG   RIGHT

3.14A

envelope surfaces (the surfaces where heat is lost) causes a continuous circulation of air. The illustration further shows that, since air cannot flow through a solid wall or a closed door, a person in an adjacent closed room is likely to be cold. Since warm, buoyant air flows primarily along the ceiling, and cool, dense air primarily drifts along the floor, a wall with gaps at top and bottom will have virtually no retarding effect on the circulation! Thus, an adjacent room can still retain visual privacy yet share the heat.

Illustration 3.14B shows just how discriminating air can be. Air is very firm about this; warm air will rise, but it will not fall! A wood stove in a split-level house must be placed at the lower level. If the stove were placed at the upper level, a person at the lower level would literally be neck-deep in a cold air pond.

A two-story house has even greater elevation relief and, as one might expect, presents worse wood-heating problems than the split level. As Illustration 3.14C shows, the only air that will flow down to the first floor is cold air—air that has already given up its heat to the outside walls. With a second-story stove installation, the first story becomes a very deep and very cold pool. (The most dramatic illustration I've heard of this phenomenon came from my neighbor who installed a wood stove on his second story. One very cold night soon thereafter, while the stove maintained 70° in the upper story, he was alarmed to hear an unfamiliar sound while using the darkened downstairs bathroom—his toilet had frozen over!)

On the other hand, properly adjusting floor registers directly above a wood stove on a lower floor, plus providing return routes for cooled air, can result in uniform heating of both floors. In fact, it is possible with register adjustments to make either floor the warmer one as desired.

I include Illustration 3.14D for ski-chalet lovers who, for whatever reason, sleep in lofts. In case you haven't already discovered this, the stove should be located under the loft rather than under the cathedral ceiling. Otherwise the heat will rise straight to the ceiling, resulting in a hot loft and cold first floor. A ceiling fan directly over the stove can overpower Nature, however, and mix the air uniformly.

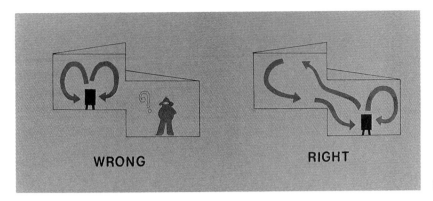

WRONG   RIGHT

3.14B

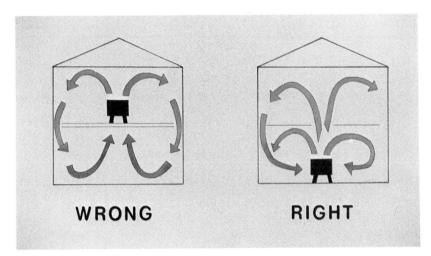

WRONG   RIGHT

3.14C

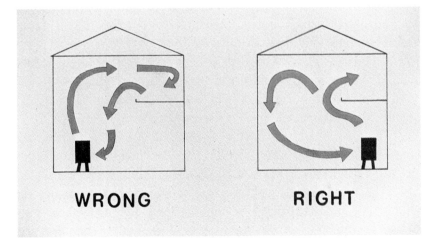

WRONG   RIGHT

3.14D

Now that we've tested our understanding of natural warm-air flow, let's consider the wood-stove installation in my house. This house falls in the category of Illustration 3.14C. Therefore, I plan to install floor registers in each upstairs room as close as possible to the wood stove below. In the case of the two bedrooms of the main house, the ideal location is directly above the wood stove in the living room. The master bedroom is above the kitchen in the ell. There, the best I can do is install an extra-large register at the closest possible point — where the ell and main house join. For the bathroom, there is little hope of satisfaction because I like my bathroom warmer than the other rooms, and I like privacy, which would, of course, be violated by a foot-square hole through the floor to the living-dining room below. The solution for the upstairs bathroom is an electric radiant heater on a timer switch.

So far, we've provided for warm air rising; now, what about cool air falling? As it happens, the return paths are already built in! The front stairway at the north end and the back stairway at the south end are perfectly placed to complete the convective loops.

Wood-Stove Safety

"Wood-stove–related fires" are caused by wood-stove operators, not by faulty wood stoves. Of course, there are exceptions, but most fires associated with wood stoves are due to improper installation. Illustration 3.15 indicates the more salient points in a safe installation.

Chimney. The chimney to which a woodstove is connected should be physically sound and lined. It is amazing how few people check the chimney all the way from basement to roof. I grant myself permission to repeat a story from *From the Walls In:* "... the fire department arrived at [a] house that was engulfed in flames. After the fire had burned itself out, there stood a wood stove, but where was the chimney? This puzzled both the owner and the chief until the owner allowed as how he didn't recall ever seeing a chimney on his house anyway! Apparently there had once been a chimney, subsequently

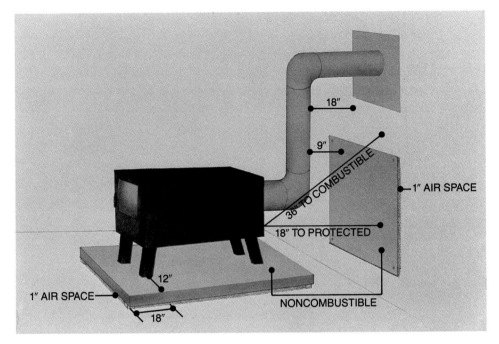

18″

9″

36″ TO COMBUSTIBLE

1″ AIR SPACE

18″ TO PROTECTED

12″

1″ AIR SPACE

18″

NONCOMBUSTIBLE

3.15

removed. The space formerly occupied by the chimney had been converted to a closet, but the metal thimble in the plaster wall had never been removed. The owner, in anticipation of the joys of woodburning, had simply hooked the stove up to the closet and kindled a roaring blaze."

There are numerous options for lining a chimney. Check with local masons and chimney sweeps for the cost and appropriateness of different options.

Stove Pipe. Consider using heavy-gauge galvanized pipe; it often outlasts the normal thinner-gauge blue-steel variety by a factor of ten (blue steel pipes should be replaced every year or two). The pipe should be installed with no more than two 90° elbows between stove and chimney and the pipe should slope slightly but continuously upward in order not to discourage the all-important chimney draft. All joints in the pipe should be secured with three sheet-metal screws. Sections of pipe should be installed in what may appear to be the upside-down position (upper pipe fitting into the lower pipe) and with the pipe seam toward the ceiling so that the inevitable creosote runs back into the stove rather than onto the floor.

Clearance. The following clearances are intended to prevent a stove fire from becoming an open fire involving your house and furnishings:

• The stove back, top, and sides should be 36″ from an unprotected surface, or 18″ from a protected surface. ("Protected" means shielded by a noncombustible material such as metal or cement-asbestos board spaced with at least 1″ of free air flow between. It does *not* mean merely surfaced with brick, since brick conducts heat fairly well.)

• The stove pipe should be 18″ from an unprotected surface (9″ from a protected surface).

• A noncombustible floor covering should extend 12″ to the sides and rear, and 18″ in front of the loading side of the stove. (The code is less clear on the nature of the floor covering, but I installed a 1″ thick piece of slate with a 1″ air space beneath.)

Smoke Detectors. Just in case! Smoke detectors are cheap. Install these early warning devices near or on the ceiling outside every sleeping area of the house. Test each smoke detector on the first day of each month and replace the batteries on New Year's Day. You should also inform your insurance company of your installation of both the stove and the smoke detectors.

Inspection. If inspection of wood-stove hookups by the fire department isn't already mandatory in your area, request a voluntary one. The feeling is like having your underwear inspected by a stranger, but it's a hell of a lot better than standing in your PJ's and bare feet watching your house go up in flames!

Backup Heat   I've heated with wood for a long time, and can honestly say that the only unpleasant aspect I've had to endure is a lack of backup heat. The bark, the ashes, the sweat and toil—that's how you know you're still alive in this age of plastic. But returning home to frozen pipes and a frozen house constitutes unreasonable cruelty.

I noted in Chapter 1 the existence of a modern, high-quality, oil-burning warm-air furnace in the basement. This I regard as a sign—a reward for the pain endured in all my previous wood-heated homes. I'm hooking it up to a clock thermostat. I think I'll set it at 50° for most of the day—but 75°, perhaps 80°, for 6 A.M.!

4. Oil and Gas Furnaces and Boilers

INTRODUCTION   In the last chapter we found that nearly all heating systems involve the same three processes of combustion, conversion, and distribution. But we also found that the cost of heat delivered to the living space could vary widely, as a function of fuel price, fuel energy content, and heating system efficiency. Using national average fuel prices and nominal system efficiencies, we examined the projected life-cycle cost of each type of system for our house. We found that wood heat would be a good solution for our house, largely due to low fuel price. We chose to retain the existing oil warm-air furnace as a backup system.

Most homeowners, however, will not choose wood; they will stick with their present oil or gas furnace or boiler. For that reason, we devote this chapter to the retrofit and proper operation of oil and gas systems.

Heating systems are remarkably like automobiles. Looking beyond minor physical differences, such as wheels and headlights, the automotive goal is to maximize *miles per gallon;* the heating goal is to maximize heating *degree days per gallon* (degree days are a measure of average difference between temperatures inside and outside). These goals are accomplished in both cases through a combination of good operating habits, proper maintenance, and up-to-date equipment. In this chapter we'll consider five low-cost ways to save fuel dollars through better operating and maintenance habits and five substantial equipment retrofits that can maximize your degree days per gallon.

Before considering how to make your heating system work better, you need to know how it works in the first place. At the risk of repeating some of what you learned in the last chapter, let's look inside oil and gas boilers and furnaces.

Oil Boiler (Illustration 4.1.).   An oil burner is similar to the carburetor of an automobile. Liquid fuel oil is pumped at constant pressure through a small pipe in the blast tube to a nozzle at the end. The size of the hole in the nozzle determines the rate of oil consumption in gallons per hour. The internal configuration of the nozzle determines the pattern of the resulting spray of oil droplets. At the same time, the burner blower (fan) draws air through an adjustable burner air inlet and forces it down the concentric blast tube and out the burner-end cone to mix turbulently with the oil droplets.

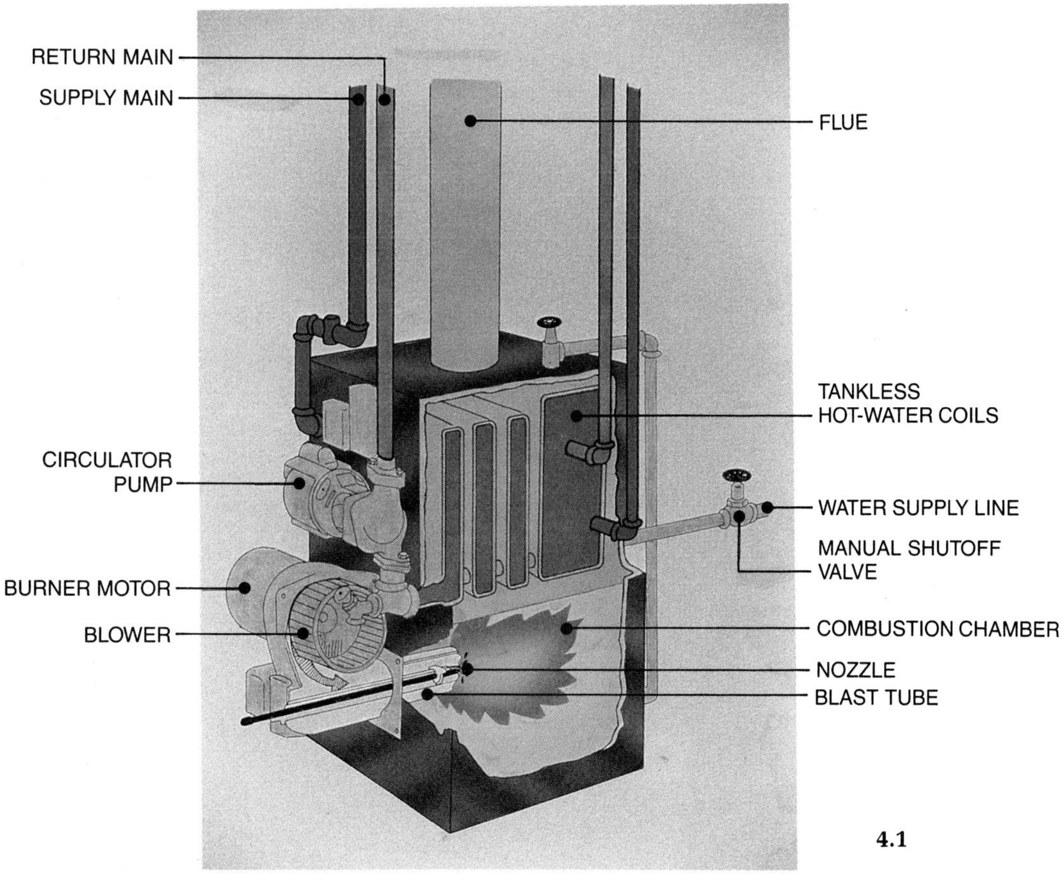

HOW HEATING SYSTEMS WORK

RETURN MAIN
SUPPLY MAIN
FLUE
TANKLESS HOT-WATER COILS
CIRCULATOR PUMP
WATER SUPPLY LINE
MANUAL SHUTOFF VALVE
BURNER MOTOR
COMBUSTION CHAMBER
BLOWER
NOZZLE
BLAST TUBE

4.1

An electric arc across two electrodes at the nozzle ignites the highly combustible mixture of air and oil, filling the combustion chamber with flame.

All components are designed with one goal in mind—maximum combustion efficiency. That goal is reached by achieving complete combustion of the oil with just the right amount of air: too little air leaves unburned oil; too much air dilutes and cools the flue gases. Complete combustion is also promoted by the proper combination of burner-end cone, nozzle, and combustion chamber. All are sized and shaped to fill the combustion chamber completely with the hottest flame possible. Therefore, changing one component may require changing the others as well.

Before departing the boiler or furnace, the hot (2,000° F) flue gases pass through a heat exchanger, the purpose of which is to extract as much heat as possible from the flue gases and pass it to a distribution medium. In a boiler, that medium is water, which can be sent through the house as water or as steam. In the most efficient systems hot water is distributed around the house by one or more circulator pumps (Illustration 4.1).

Most of the cost difference between boilers is in the effectiveness of the heat exchanger. Obviously, heat exchangers with larger surface areas are more efficient at extracting heat from the flue gases. Wet-base boilers, in which the heat exchanger actually surrounds the combustion chamber, tend to be both more expensive and more efficient than dry-base boilers.

After traversing the heat exchanger, the cooled (still $300^{+°}$) flue gases exit by way of a flue pipe to the chimney and the outdoors. On their way out of the flue pipe, they pass a rather intriguing device called a barometric damper. As we learned in the previous chapter, warm air rises. The buoyancy of a column of air is proportional to its height and the difference in temperature between it and the surrounding air. With a chimney height of 20 to 40 feet and temperature differences of hundreds of degrees, the suction caused by this "chimney effect" is powerful. Unfortunately, the amount of suction varies with outdoor temperature and velocity of wind over the chimney, and tends to be greatest on cold and windy days. This suction pulls air into the burner air inlets and through the burner, combustion chamber, and heat exchanger, with two deleterious effects: (1) the precise air-oil combustion balance established by the service technician is disturbed; and (2) valuable heat is continually robbed from the heat exchanger during burner-off periods. The purpose of the hinged and weighted barometric damper is to introduce air between the heating system and the chimney in such a way that the suction through the burner air inlet remains minimal and constant.

Finally, to operate this system, which is so automobile-like, we need to find the throttle. The output of heat may actually be controlled by *two* thermostats. The first is the familiar wall-mounted unit located in the space to be warmed. It signals the heating system whenever heat is desired. The second thermostat, in the case of a boiler with a tankless water-heating coil, is called an aquastat. It holds the water stored in the boiler heat exchanger to a narrow range of temperatures so that hot water will be instantly available when called for. It is this second thermostat that actually controls the burner.

In a steam boiler without a tankless hot-water coil there is no aquastat. The house thermostat starts the burner, which generates steam. If more steam is generated than required to satisfy the radiators, a steam pressure switch turns the burner off. When the house thermostat is satisfied, the burner also stops and the boiler cools down. Of course it doesn't get too cool in winter because of the frequency of the thermostat calls.

Oil Furnace (Illustration 4.2). A warm-air furnace differs from a boiler principally in its heat exchanger and distribution medium. The medium that carries heat to the house from a furnace is ordinary air. Since the heat exchanger is not subject to either pressure or corrosion from water, it can be lighter and easier to fabricate and therefore less expensive.

The furnace also has a second thermostat, in this case a

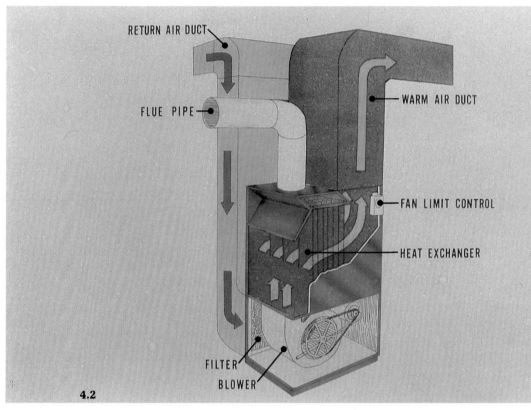

RETURN AIR DUCT

FLUE PIPE

WARM AIR DUCT

FAN LIMIT CONTROL

HEAT EXCHANGER

FILTER

BLOWER

4.2

complicated three-switch device called the fan limit switch. This triple thermostat and the room thermostat interrelate in the following ways:

1. When the furnace is off, it's at the temperature of its surroundings (unlike the boiler with the tankless coil).
2. The room temperature drops and the room thermostat calls for heat.
3. The burner starts to heat the furnace heat exchanger.
4. As soon as the heat exchanger reaches the fan "on" temperature, the blower begins to deliver warm air to the living space.
5. As soon as the heat exchanger reaches its temperature limit, the high limit switch turns the burner off.
6. The blower continues to deliver warm air (cooling the heat exchanger) until the heat exchanger reaches the fan-off temperature.

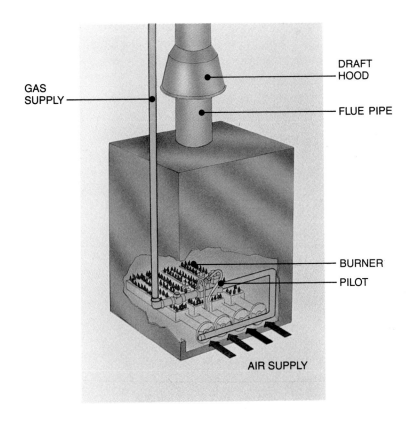

GAS
SUPPLY

DRAFT
HOOD

FLUE PIPE

BURNER

PILOT

AIR SUPPLY

4.3

Gas Boiler and Furnace (Illustration 4.3). The primary difference between gas and oil heating systems involves the handling of the fuel. Most gas systems in use today utilize "atmospheric burners." These are no more complicated than the burners in a gas range, just larger. Complete combustion is ensured simply by supplying an ample—indeed, excessive—amount of air. As in the common older kitchen range, a gas pilot light stands eternally ready (and eternally wasting gas) to ignite the burner whenever the room thermostat activates the gas-release control.

Some improvements found in modern gas furnaces and boilers make them much more like their oil counterparts: controlling the air-gas mixture with a pressurizing blower, and igniting the flame electrically.

Heat Distribution. I have purposely delayed discussing the methods of distributing the heat to the house in order to concentrate better on the more complex processes of combustion and conversion. Now we can discuss distribution independently of fuel type.

Illustration 4.4 shows a hydronic, or hot-water, distribution system. Hot water (usually between 160° and 200°) is forced by a circulator pump through finned sections of pipe in baseboard heating units that release the heat. Cast-iron radiators can also sometimes be used. After giving up a portion of the heat, the water returns to the heat exchanger to pick up more heat.

The distribution of heat can be controlled through the use of separate zones (separate loops of pipe with separate circulating pumps and thermostats), or a single pump with different zone valves. Each zone is controlled by its own thermostat. Although the finned sections of convector pipe are more efficient at transferring heat, bare distribution pipes give off significant heat as well, and should be insulated except where located within the heated space.

Illustration 4.5 shows a warm-air distribution system. Since air carries much less heat per volume than water, an air distribution system requires relatively large ducts. Warm air from the heat exchanger is forced by the furnace blower through supply ducts to the remote areas of the living space. The warm-air outlet registers are usually located on the cold outside walls. The cooled air is then collected through one or more centrally located return registers and returned to the heat exchanger through the return duct. Note that the air travels in an open loop. In other words, the air finds its own way from outlet to return registers. This requires some thought on the part of the installer in order to achieve uniform heating. Fine-tuning is accomplished by using adjustable dampers in the individual supply ducts.

Domestic Hot Water. Oil and gas boilers resemble hot-water heaters in operation. In fact, I know one person who heats his small, well-insulated home by running a loop of pipe from an oil-fired domestic hot-water heater to a baseboard.

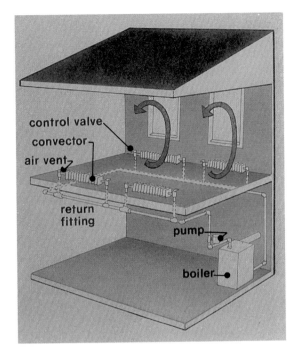

control valve
convector
air vent
return fitting
pump
boiler

4.4

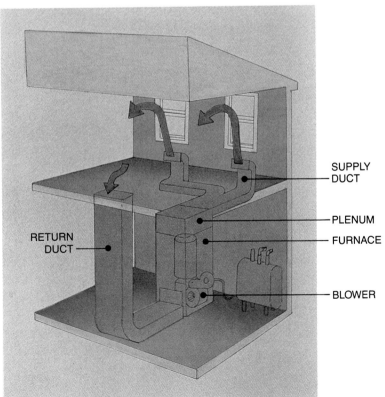

SUPPLY DUCT
PLENUM
FURNACE
RETURN DUCT
BLOWER

4.5

Taking advantage of the similarity of operation and function, boilers are often equipped with "tankless water heaters"—coils of copper tubing immersed inside the heat exchanger (a heat exchanger within a heat exchanger). Since only a few additional coils of copper tubing are involved, the incremental cost is less than that for separate space and domestic water heaters.

The efficiency of a tankless water heater is identical to that of the space-heating system during the heating season. During the summer, however, the boiler capacity is woefully mismatched to the hot-water demand (like mowing a lawn with a chain saw), and the efficiency drops severely. When both winter and summer operations are combined, the overall efficiency of a tankless system can be as low as 30 to 40 percent!

WHERE THE ENERGY GOES

So far, we have focused on how well furnaces and boilers work. Did you assume that all of the energy in the fuel gets to the living space? This, unfortunately, is not the case. Most heating systems resemble the antiquated Boston water system—about half of the water that enters the system cannot be accounted for as it leaks and dribbles from the myriad ancient subterranean water pipes. The difference between the energy locked in the fuel we buy and the heat delivered from it obviously indicates that a valuable resource is wasted beneath our very noses! Most of the retrofit technology described below is designed to recover some portion of this waste. Before tackling specific measures, let's consider where the energy goes.

Illustration 4.6 shows that the energy contained in the fuel ends up in one of three broad categories:

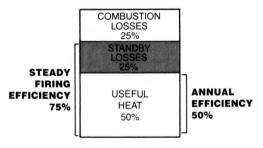

4.6

• **Combustion losses** typically account for about 25 percent of the fuel energy. These include the energy lost through improper burner adjustment (incomplete combustion due to too little air, or heat dilution due to excessive air), heat not extracted by the heat exchanger and lost up the stack, and the latent heat contained in the water vapor produced by combustion. The latter two components amount to a theoretical minimum 13 percent loss in oil systems, due to the need to discharge the moist and corrosive flue gases at more than 250° to the atmosphere.

• **Standby losses** are those incurred not only during actual combustion, but during burner-off periods as well. They include jacket losses (from heat exchanger to surroundings), stack losses (through the heat exchanger up the stack), and distribution losses (from hydronic piping or warm-air ducting to unheated spaces). Note that jacket and distribution losses are eliminated merely by including the heating system within the thermal envelope—a powerful argument for insulating basement walls!

• **Useful heat** is the residual energy that manages, despite our criminal neglect, to find its way to the living space. Over the entire heating season the typical useful heat from an older system amounts to only 50 to 60 percent of the energy we purchase. The difference between that and the theoretical maximum of 87 percent for oil and 93 percent for gas shows how rewarding retrofit can be.

SAVINGS DUE TO OPERATING ADJUSTMENTS

Below are listed five different ways to maintain and operate heating systems more efficiently. None costs more than $50; all except the last can be done by a reasonably skilled homeowner.

• **Thermostat Setback.** The rate at which a building loses heat is proportional to the difference in temperature between inside and outside. Obviously there are two ways to minimize this difference: (1) move to a warmer climate, or (2) lower the thermostat. Over the entire heating season the average indoor to outdoor temperature difference is surprisingly small (about 30°) in the northern half of the United States. Therefore, a small thermostat setback can result in a large saving. Illustration 4.7 shows the approximate savings that you could get in any

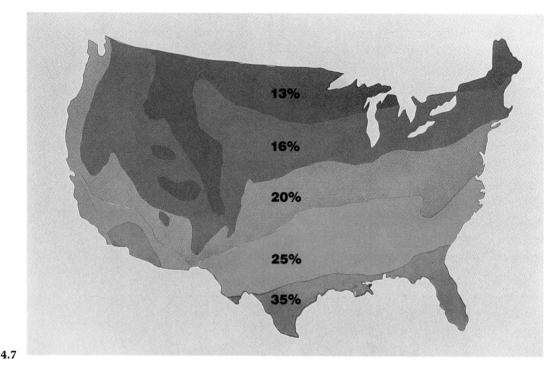

4.7

Heating Savings for a Five-Degree Setback

location in the United States for each degree you permanently lower your thermostat. For example, permanently lowering a thermostat in Boston by 1° would save about 3 percent, and by 5° about 15 percent, of the heating bill.

As a rule of thumb temporary setbacks save a fraction of the permanent setback savings shown in the illustration, proportional to the duration of the setback; i.e., an eight-hour setback would save roughly one-third as much as a permanent (twenty-four-hour) setback. Many people already achieve these savings by manually setting back the thermostat. Others install clock thermostats that not only never forget, but save their masters the misery of arriving home to or getting up in a cold house.

• **Fan and Aquastat Low Limit.** System standby losses are similar to building heat losses in that they are proportional to the difference in temperatures between the system and its surroundings. The temperature of a system is maintained by either a fan limit switch (furnace) or aquastat (boiler).

Lowering the fan-off temperature setting to room temperature means the blower will extract every Btu of useful heat from the furnace before it shuts off. (Since moving air has a chilling effect on the body, room temperature plus ten degrees is probably a more practical goal).

The low-limit aquastat setting of a boiler with tankless domestic hot water obviously cannot be lowered to room temperature, because there would often be no hot water at the tap. However, the setting can be lowered seasonally by the same number of degrees the outside warms up. For example, assume your aquastat is presently set to operate between 180° and 200° (there are two settings, "lo" and "hi"), and your annual minimum outside temperature is 0°. In the spring and fall, when you expect overnight lows of 30°, your boiler will still provide adequate heat if set back by 30° to 150° and 170°. Your standby losses, however, will be reduced proportionally!

• **Replacement of Furnace Filter.** Furnaces contain one or more air filters in the cold-air return duct just above the blower. Filters perform the wonderful service of removing dust that otherwise would be deposited on your furniture and under your bed. They also clog rapidly. A clogged filter forces the blower to run longer to deliver the same amount of heat, which in turn means a longer duration of standby loss, as well as unnecessary consumption of electricity. Furnace filters can be vacuumed with an ordinary household vacuum cleaner. They also cost about fifty cents apiece. Vacuum or replace them once a month.

• **Burner Tune-up.** The overall efficiency of your system is actually maximized when burner air input and combustion efficiency are slightly restricted. As a result, a small amount of unburned oil escapes as soot and is deposited on the surfaces of the heat exchanger. Over time, the buildup of soot insulates those surfaces and reduces the efficiency of the heat exchange. An oil burner "tune-up" includes cleaning the heat exchanger, as well as adjusting the air-oil mixture for optimum efficiency. Let experience be your guide, but start with a yearly tune-up. Gas systems produce less soot and therefore require less servicing.

• **Decrease in Nozzle Size.** Earlier, we distinguished between combustion (burner-on) losses and standby (burner-off) losses. Maximum overall or annual efficiency is achieved by maximizing your furnace's on-time and minimizing its off-time. The idea is the same as in driving an automobile: the best mileage is obtained by a steady pressure applied as if there were an egg between your foot and the gas pedal. In a heating system this is achieved by reducing the nozzle size and fuel flow rate to the minimum required just to heat the house on the coldest night. To find out how much to reduce your nozzle size, time the burner on that coldest night. If it runs 30 minutes out of each hour, your nozzle size could be reduced by as much as 50 percent, provided that this is not less than the minimum design flow rate for your system.

SAVINGS DUE TO EQUIPMENT MODIFICATIONS

Beyond the simple and low-cost fixes there are five substantial equipment modifications or additions that, in most cases, can retrofit your present system to a modern standard of efficiency.

• **Flame-Retention-Head Oil Burner.** If you presently burn oil in a nonretention-head burner, run, don't walk, to your oil dealer! This type of burner, available for the past ten years, should save you between 10 percent and 20 percent of your fuel bill. It saves in two ways: (1) the vaned head mixes oil and air more completely for maximum combustion efficiency with minimum air; and (2) the burner blower operates at high speed and pressure, requiring smaller air inlet holes and resulting in smaller standby losses up the chimney. In some of the latest models the burner air inlets open only during combustion, totally eliminating the stack standby loss.

• **Automatic Vent Damper.** This is an electrically operated solid damper (disk) placed in the flue pipe between the barometric damper and the chimney. It opens just before combustion to let flue gases escape, and closes a short time after combustion to reduce the standby flow of air through the heat exchanger and loss of building air through the barometric damper.

About 5 percent of the disk is left open in order to guarantee that residual fumes will still escape up the chimney. Unfortunately, this opening limits the reduction in stack loss to about 50 percent of the present loss.

Some oil dealers are reluctant to install these devices, feeling they may increase the number of service calls. Fortunately, the flame-retention-head burner accomplishes the same purpose, largely eliminating the need for an oil-vent damper.

A typical gas system has, instead of a barometric damper, a draft hood to admit air and hold the burner inlet air flow constant. A vent damper installed between draft load and chimney will thus result in a reduction in the volume of house air escaping up the chimney and a diversion of residual furnace heat from the flue into the room. If the gas system is located in (and draws its combustion air from) a purposely heated space, then both effects result in fuel savings; otherwise they are meaningless.

The bottom line is: for oil, get a retention-head burner; for gas, get a vent damper if your furnace is located in a heated space.

• **Boiler Modulating Control.** Also known as a variable aquastat, this computer-like device accomplishes automatically what you might do manually in setting back a boiler aquastat low-limit switch. It constantly measures outdoor temperature and adjusts the aquastat setting so that the boiler and distribution system are only as hot as required to heat the house. All system standby losses are thus reduced.

A clock-driven override is usually included for tankless systems to boost the boiler temperature at preselected times of hot-water use.

• **Electric Ignition.** The pilot flame in the typical gas system consumes gas at the rate of 70 CCF (or 70 therms) per year. Of course the pilot could be shut off during the nonheating portion of the year, and pilot heat does contribute to space heating during burner-on times. Replacing the pilot flame with an electric ignition could save, therefore, between 0 and 70 CCF of gas per year. Since pilots are typically left on year-round, savings are potentially greatest in the South.

• **All-New System.** Your present system may just be plumb tuckered out. Or it may look like a snowman (a sure sign it once burned coal and is, therefore, not a prime candidate for retrofit). If either description applies to your system, then consider installing a whole new system. You'll be buying all of the improvements listed above at a bargain price.

By law, all new systems now carry an efficiency label. The AFUE (Annual Fuel Utilization Efficiency) is the predicted annual efficiency of the particular system if installed at the proper firing rate and if operated under ideal conditions. Like the EPA miles per gallon figures on new automobiles, use it to compare models, not to plan your fuel budget! It is an indicator of quality and operating economy.

ALL TOGETHER NOW! — THE INTERACTIVE EFFECT

Many of the devices described above act to save the same heat in different ways. Since the same heat can't be saved twice, we should be aware that the savings are interactive. As a rule of thumb, retention-head burners, vent dampers, and boiler-modulating controls each save about 50 percent of system standby losses when installed alone.

Two installed together (provided both are appropriate to the system) would then save an initial 50 percent, plus a second 50 percent of the remaining 50 percent, for a total of 75 percent of the existing loss. All three (or a brand-new system) would save roughly 50 + 25 + 12 = 87 percent of the existing losses.

Illustration 4.8 shows step by step how a typical system could be improved to yield as much as 83 percent useful heat, starting from only 50 percent. I have listed the steps from left to right in their most cost-effective order; proceeding from left to right should yield the greatest savings for the smallest investment. I must stress, however, that all of the projected savings above are typical figures. Your savings might be greater or smaller.

Need I remind you that, just as there is no typical person, there is no *typical system*? Discuss *your* system with your fuel dealer.

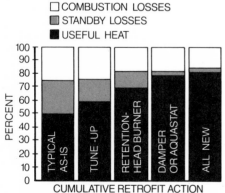

WHERE THE HEAT GOES
☐ COMBUSTION LOSSES
▨ STANDBY LOSSES
■ USEFUL HEAT

CUMULATIVE RETROFIT ACTION

4.8

5. Heat from the Sun

In the last two chapters we've discussed methods of heating with conventional fuels. In Chapter 3 I convinced myself (at least) to install a wood stove for primary heating and to retain the existing oil furnace as a backup. And in Chapter 4 I described how to optimize the efficiencies of gas and oil furnaces and boilers.

My projected heating bill of about $470 for five cords of wood is not large. But I'm the sort of person who just can't pass up a freebie. I once had a sailboat, and when the wind died and I *had* to get somewhere (sailors are always going somewhere; they have to justify owning a boat!) I'd start the engine; but I'd also keep the sail hoisted just on the chance of a puff of air.

Sunshine is to a house as wind is to a boat — free energy. But if you've ever been a sailor, you know that sailing doesn't just happen! Getting to your port involves keeping an eye to the weather, and shifting and tacking in constant response to the vagaries of the wind. Heating with the sun involves just such a sensitivity to the weather: starting fires; not starting fires if the sky is lightening; opening or closing shutters, depending on whether the sun is shining, and from what quadrant. If your only purpose is to get there, drive; but if you want to participate in the journey, sail. Likewise, if you just want to get through the winter, set your thermostat at 70°; if you want to experience the seasons, use the sun. I'm of the latter persuasion and so this chapter is all about setting your sails to capture free solar heat.

Passive Solar — A Definition. First I must make a distinction. Lots of people think of rooftop collectors, pipes, and storage tanks in the basement when they hear the word "solar." That's *active solar heating*. A second kind is *passive solar heating*—using ordinary windows to collect, and window insulation to retain, just the right amount of solar radiation to heat (but not overheat) your little vessel. You can probably tell that I favor passive over active. Yup, *passive solar for active people*—that's me.

EXPECTATIONS   Before charging ahead, blinded by our enthusiasm for solar energy, let's keep ourselves honest by listing our expectations. Like any other energy feature of the house, our solar alternatives should be examined in the harsh light of expected functions. Perhaps, indeed, the original farmer-builder of my house was right in positioning it to face the street to the north! You may or may not share all of the expectations, but here is my personal list:

5.1

• **Lower the fuel bill** (Illustration 5.1). It's not difficult actually to *increase*, rather than decrease, your fuel bill by the addition of glazing. I want passive solar to pay me back, in terms of fuel savings.

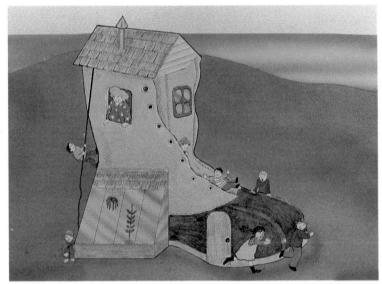

5.2

• **Add living space** (Illustration 5.2). The Old Woman in the Shoe would find, as so many have, that a sunspace is a delightful place for children to play or moms and dads to eat Sunday brunch. Personally, I'd settle for a passive solar glazing that made an existing space more pleasant.

5.3

• **Relieve cabin fever** (Illustration 5.3). Put some sand on the floor, Hawaiian music on the phono, and a piña colada in your hand, and a sunspace is a fair substitute for a trip to Florida.

5.4

• **Not overheat** (Illustration 5.4). Of course you can overdo it! Before the age of computers, and with a noteworthy lack of common sense, I built a house that achieved 90° by 10 A.M. on clear winter days. Excess heat is worthless heat. And since it is gained through excess windows, it spells excess nighttime loss.

5.5

• **Not overcool** (Illustration 5.5). The corollary of the above, it is achieved by not going overboard at a glass sale, and by insulating those windows at night.

• **Be maintenance-free** (Illustration 5.6). Of course you can build a $5 greenhouse! For plans, consult back issues of *The Mother Earth News*.

THE WATER BUCKET —A PASSIVE SOLAR ANALOGY

Heat loss, solar gain, diurnal swing, thermal mass, auxiliary heat—the technical jargon surrounding passive solar heating discourages, rather than invites, understanding. If not arrested in time, it often leads to extravagant hand-waving, even by its practitioners, rather than serious design consideration.

I find, however, that a remarkable analogy can be drawn between the behavior of a solar-heated building and a water-filled bucket. You may have given up splashing about in buckets and building dams in your parents' driveway long ago, but surely you retain an understanding of water and leaky buckets!

Illustration 5.7 shows the analogy. The bucket is the house (more specifically the thermal envelope of the house). The water in the bucket is the heat in the house. The level of water in the bucket is the level of temperature inside the house versus outdoors. A water leak in the bucket is a heat leak in the house.

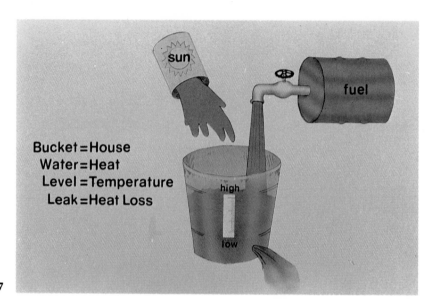

Bucket = House
Water = Heat
Level = Temperature
Leak = Heat Loss

5.7

Thrown into the bucket on a random schedule is a random amount of water from a can labeled "sun," obviously representing the rather unpredictable but substantial heating effect of sunshine through windows. Finally, there is also a drum with a spigot from which water can be drawn at will, representing addition of heat to the house from a conventional heating system.

If you were a child instructed to design and operate a game involving a water bucket, a can of sunshine, and a drum of fuel, with the goal of always maintaining the water level between high and low marks — but using a minimum amount of water from the spigot — I daresay you'd have no problem. By trial and error, if not by intuition, you'd:

1. plug the hole in the bucket;
2. paint the "high" and "low" marks as high and low as possible on the bucket;
3. use a washtub instead of a bucket (large surface area compared to height);
4. use a "sun" can of volume just equaling the amount of water between the low and high marks on the bucket.

By analogy, in a passive solar house you'd be:

1. insulating, caulking, and weatherstripping;
2. letting the temperature swing as much as comfort and a sweater allow;
3. incorporating a large thermal mass, such as masonry floor and walls, so that the house could absorb and release much heat with minimal temperature change;
4. adding just enough solar glazing so that the solar gain on a clear winter day raises the house temperature from the overnight low thermostat setting to the highest temperature you can tolerate without opening a window.

The name of this game is passive solar heating—minimizing your fuel bill by working with the sun.

Over the years people have tried hundreds of variations on this game. Four generic variations have proved successful:

VARIATIONS ON THE THEME

day night

STORED HEAT

5.8

• **Direct Gain** (Illustration 5.8). The most popular and cost-effective strategy simply recognizes that few solar collectors are more efficient at collecting solar energy than ordinary south-facing windows. For no extra cost the usual complement of windows can be reoriented to south. The ordinary light wood-frame house has limited ability to absorb heat. If too great an area of glazing is installed, the house overheats on clear days, requiring wasteful venting of excess heat. The main design concern here is providing the proper ratio of "thermal mass" to glazing area. Use the "Rule of Thumb for Thermal Mass" (page 74) as a guide.

With the proper amount of thermal mass, just enough solar radiation is converted to heated air in striking lightweight surfaces and furnishings to heat the house during the day. The remaining fraction of solar energy goes into storage by sinking into massive materials, such as a concrete slab, masonry walls, or even double-sheetrocked walls, from which it later emerges as a nocturnal heat supply.

Of course the amount of heat that must be gained and stored daily equals the amount of daily heat loss, and so direct-gain houses are usually very tight and well insulated. This pertains particularly to the glazing. Except in the sunniest and warmest areas of the country, the fuel reduction resulting from uninsulated glazings is very close to nothing. Therefore, movable window insulations such as shades or shutters are a must (see Chapter 7 for the options).

In the summer, solar gain is unwanted. Although the same window insulation could be used to block the radiation (creating a cavelike ambience), better solutions for summer shading are: (1) deciduous trees, such as maples and oaks, and (2) in lieu of trees, a roof overhang or awning.

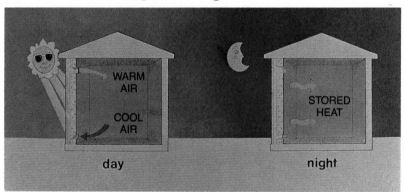

5.9

• **Masonry Wall** (Illustration 5.9). Also known as a Trombé wall in honor of its most famous practitioner, Felix Trombé, this version of the game takes advantage of a natural phenomenon long favored by snakes—the ability of stonelike materials slowly to absorb and release large quantities of heat.

During the day solar radiation streams through an outer double glazing and strikes the dark surface of a solid masonry wall. Masonry is not a good insulator (one inch of fiberglass insulates as well as 3 feet of masonry), but the masonry stores heat so well that the resulting heat wave travels through the wall at a rate of only one inch per hour. The peak temperature at the outer surface is reached around midday and may be as high as 150° At one inch per hour, the temperature peaks on the living space side of the wall at around 8 P.M. for an 8″ thick wall and midnight for a 12″ wall. The heat diffuses on the way, so that the peak living side wall temperature is only around 80°.

Placing vents totaling about 6 percent of the entire masonry wall area both high and low (3 percent each) in the wall allows daytime heating by convection. This also has the advantage of reducing the surface temperature, which reduces heat flow back through the glazing and increases overall efficiency. Therefore, the masonry wall heats both day and night.

Although high levels of building insulation are recommended, the use of night window insulation is not common in masonry wall. Dampers of very thin plastic, such as 1-mil Mylar, prevent reverse convection at night, and the wall itself acts as night window insulation. Real insulation is preferable, but obviously difficult to install and operate.

5.10

• **Water Wall** (Illustration 5.10). At first glance this design, with its massive water containers placed between glazing and living space, appears to be similar to the masonry wall. But there are significant differences.

First, heat absorbed by the water does not travel in a wave, but is mixed rapidly and uniformly by convection (like convection of room air around a stove). Therefore, water-container surface temperatures are reduced, which reduces heat loss back through the glazing and increases efficiency.

Second, the water can be clear, in which case it transmits considerable light and daytime heat directly to the living space, or it can be dyed to absorb any fraction desired. In another version, not shown, an ordinary stud wall is simply filled with water containers.

Most often, the water containers stand well within the building and night window insulation is lowered to prevent night heat loss.

5.11

• **Sunspace** (Illustration 5.11). Sunspaces make a lot more sense to me than either masonry walls or water walls. A snakelike proclivity makes me want to crawl into that warm space between glazing and heat storage wall. Simply moving the glazing out about ten feet provides a wonderful warm sunny room and still performs the function of reducing the fuel bill.

Although Illustration 5.11 shows a masonry rear wall, the same sunspace could be added to a wood frame wall. In that case, the sunspace would perform much like a direct-gain system. In both cases, the sunspace is too small to absorb all of the solar gain, so some means should be provided to share the heat with the adjacent living space. If the sunspace spans two stories, a door on the first floor and one or more openable windows on the second floor would suffice; otherwise a thermostatically controlled window fan and door on the first floor work well.

Some practitioners use the terms "sunspace" and "solar greenhouse" interchangeably. This is a serious mistake. The structure in Illustration 5.11 could be used as either, but not both. The purpose of a sunspace is to provide a warm, dry sunny space and deliver excess heat to the adjacent structure. The purpose of a greenhouse is to grow plants in a sunny but moist environment. Blowing moist warm air from a greenhouse into your house is equivalent to boiling maple sap in your kitchen.

Everyone knows that the sun rises in the east and sets in the west. Therefore it spends most of its time in the southern half of the sky. Just how important is it for solar glazings to face south? Illustration 5.12 shows for Portland, Maine, total winter solar gain per square foot through double-glazed windows facing eight points of the compass. The chart shows that windows facing as much as 45° away from south (southeast and southwest) still gain 80 percent of the maximum radiation. But beyond that point, radiation drops rapidly. The gain drops to 45 percent at east and west.

We see, then, how effectively windows can gain heat from the winter sun. Unfortunately, they lose heat by conduction as well. Illustration 5.13 shows the winter gain, loss, and net gain (gain minus loss) for the same windows. South-facing windows still show a net gain (although diminished by one-third), east and west windows just about break even, and windows on the north become big losers.

Windows gain solar energy for only about eight hours of the day; but they lose heat twenty-four hours around. Considerable savings can be realized by covering the windows with movable window insulation during those nonsolar sixteen hours. Illustration 5.14 shows the dramatic improvement in net gain when movable window insulation is used. South windows keep all but

PERFORMANCE

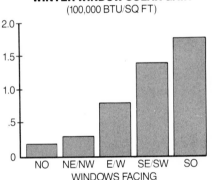

WINTER WINDOW SOLAR GAIN
(100,000 BTU/SQ FT)

WINDOWS FACING   5.12

WINTER WINDOW SOLAR BALANCE
(100,000 BTU/SQ FT)

☐ SOLAR GAIN
▨ NET GAIN
■ HEAT LOSS

WINDOWS FACING   5.13

HEAT FROM THE SUN 73

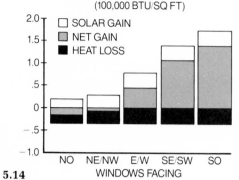

**SOLAR BALANCE
WITH WINDOW INSULATION**
(100,000 BTU/SQ FT)

□ SOLAR GAIN
▨ NET GAIN
■ HEAT LOSS

5.14

WINDOWS FACING: NO NE/NW E/W SE/SW SO

20 percent of their gain, east and west windows are now winners, and north windows show negligible losses.

All the evidence leads us to conclude that, in general, passive solar glazings should face to the south of due east and west, and should be covered with movable insulation at night. Given those conditions, what performance can we expect? Table 5.1, adapted from Volume Two of the DOE *Passive Solar Design Handbook*, gives us a pretty good idea of how high to set our sights. The first column lists the location. The second column shows the recommended ratio (fraction) of glazing area to living area as a range. The third column gives the percentage range by which the fuel bill would be lowered by adding the solar glazing ratios of column two.

As an example, let's look at the location nearest my house: Portland, Maine. The total living area of my house, counting both floors, is 1,840 square feet. The table tells me that a double-glazed and night-insulated solar glazing ranging from .17 × 1,840 = 313 sq.ft. to .34 × 1,840 = 626 sq.ft. would reduce my fuel bill by 45 percent to 69 percent. Wow! The only problem is I don't know where I'd ever install 313 square feet of glass, much less 626! But don't worry; you won't go far wrong if you interpolate between zero (zero glazing = zero savings) and the lower set of figures.

I already have 45 square feet of south and east-facing glass, and I know where I'd like to install another 120 square feet, for a total of 165. By interpolation, the table promises that 165 square feet of glazing will reduce my fuel bill by approximately

$$\frac{165 \text{ sq.ft.}}{313 \text{ sq.ft.}} \times 45\% = 24\%$$

RULE OF THUMB FOR THERMAL MASS

A thermal storage mass of 0.6 × SSF pounds of water or 3 × SSF pounds of masonry is recommended for each square foot of south glazing, where SSF is the desired solar savings fraction (in percent). This assumes that the mass is in the direct sun all day as, for example, in a water wall. In direct-gain situations this is adequate thermal storage, provided (1) the mass is within

City	Percentage of glazed area*	Percentage of reduction in fuel bill*
Alabama, Birmingham	9 – 18	34 – 58
Arizona, Phoenix	6 – 12	48 – 75
Arkansas, Little Rock	10 – 19	37 – 62
California, Los Angeles	5 – 9	44 – 72
California, San Francisco	6 – 13	45 – 71
Colorado, Denver	12 – 23	47 – 74
Connecticut, Hartford	17 – 35	40 – 64
Delaware, Wilmington	15 – 29	39 – 63
District of Columbia, Washington	12 – 23	37 – 61
Florida, Orlando	3 – 6	37 – 63
Georgia, Atlanta	8 – 17	34 – 58
Idaho, Boise	14 – 28	48 – 71
Illinois, Chicago	17 – 35	43 – 67
Indiana, Indianapolis	14 – 28	37 – 60
Iowa, Des Moines	21 – 43	50 – 75
Kansas, Topeka	14 – 28	45 – 71
Kentucky, Louisville	13 – 27	35 – 59
Louisiana, Baton Rouge	6 – 12	34 – 59
Maine, Portland	17 – 34	45 – 69
Massachusetts, Boston	15 – 29	40 – 64
Michigan, Detroit	17 – 34	39 – 61
Minnesota, Duluth	25 – 50	50 – 70
Mississippi, Jackson	8 – 15	34 – 59
Missouri, St. Louis	15 – 29	41 – 65
Montana, Great Falls	18 – 37	56 – 77
Nebraska, North Platte	17 – 34	50 – 76
Nevada, Las Vegas	9 – 18	48 – 75
New Hampshire, Concord	17 – 34	45 – 68
New Jersey, Newark	13 – 25	39 – 64
New Mexico, Albuquerque	11 – 22	46 – 73
New York, Syracuse	19 – 38	37 – 59
No. Carolina, Greensboro	10 – 20	37 – 63
No. Dakota, Bismarck	25 – 50	56 – 77
Ohio, Columbus	14 – 28	35 – 57
Oklahoma, Tulsa	11 – 22	41 – 67
Oregon, Salem	12 – 24	37 – 59
Pennsylvania, Pittsburgh	14 – 28	33 – 55
Rhode Island, Providence	15 – 30	40 – 64
So. Carolina, Columbia	8 – 17	36 – 61
So. Dakota, Pierre	22 – 43	58 – 80
Tennessee, Nashville	10 – 21	33 – 55
Texas, Dallas	8 – 17	38 – 64
Utah, Salt Lake City	13 – 26	48 – 72
Vermont, Burlington	22 – 43	46 – 68
Virginia, Richmond	11 – 22	37 – 61
Washington, Seattle	11 – 22	39 – 59
W. Virginia, Charleston	13 – 25	32 – 54
Wisconsin, Madison	20 – 40	51 – 74
Wyoming, Casper	13 – 26	53 – 78

Table 5.1
TARGET PASSIVE SOLAR HEATING PERFORMANCE

*Figures are ranges. The glazed area is a percentage of the living area.

the direct-gain space or encloses the direct-gain space; (2) the mass is not insulated from the space; and (3) the mass has an exposed surface area equal to at least 3 times the glazed area. If masonry is used, it is not effective beyond a depth of 4″. Normal house furnishings and an extra layer of gypsum drywall can each be credited as equivalent to 10 pounds of masonry per square foot of living area.

Example. Our goal is a solar savings of 24 percent with a glazed area of 165 square feet. By the rule of thumb above we should provide a thermal mass equivalent to $3 \times 24 = 72$ pounds of masonry for each square foot of glazing, or a total mass of $72 \times 165 = 11{,}880$ pounds. The furnishings allowance alone for 1,840 square feet of living space gives us $10 \times 1{,}840 = 18{,}400$ pounds; so we are not in danger of overheating.

SOLAR OPTIONS

I'm not building a *new* house. Therefore, anything I do to capture solar energy is at extra cost; and I've already stated my conviction that any solar feature will have to justify itself in terms of fuel savings.

I've identified three no-cost–low-cost modifications that promise to increase my solar gain and lower my fuel bill (Illustration 5.15):

1. *Removing the porch roof.* This would expose the east window in the kitchen and the south window in the dining room to winter sun. Since the poor roof condition requires removal or replacement for safety reasons anyway, this is a no-cost solar option.

2. *Installing patio-door replacement panels in south wall of master bedroom.* For aesthetic reasons, I'm enlarging the master bedroom by removing the existing closet and stairway hall. The added cost of the additional 36 square feet of glazing is $360, including labor.

3. *Converting the existing bay window to a "sunspace."* This can be done inexpensively by retaining the original bay foundation, floor, ceiling, and roof. Adding the maximum amount of glazing (three 34″ × 76″ and two 28″ × 76″ standard patio-door replacement panels) will cost an estimated $900.

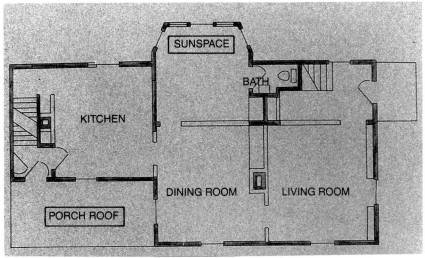

FIRST FLOOR

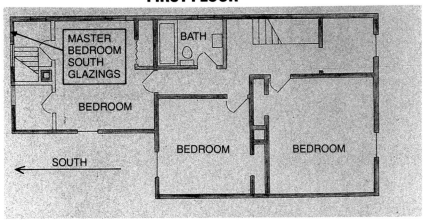

SECOND FLOOR

5.15

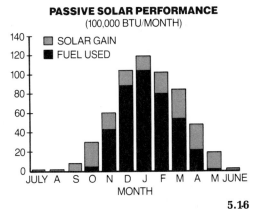

PASSIVE SOLAR PERFORMANCE
(100,000 BTU/MONTH)

5.16

Actually, I'm not comparing options; I like all three. The first option is no problem; at zero cost it pays back immediately. To investigate the others and to confirm the rough estimate from Table 5.1, I ran my altered house design through the more detailed month-by-month calculations outlined in the *Passive Solar Design Handbook*. The results, shown in Illustration 5.16, are gratifying. The twelve bars represent the energy flows during the twelve months starting in July and ending in June. The total bar height is the total heat loss of the house in 100,000 Btu per month (roughly equivalent to gallons of oil). The top of each bar represents the useful solar gain for each month in the same units. The bottom part of each bar represents the amount of heat that must be supplied by the heating system.

According to Illustration 5.16, taken all together my three "solar systems" will not only make me a happier person, but will shorten my winter by several months and, best of all, reduce my fuel bill by 28 percent, or $131 per year. At an estimated total cost of $1,260, these solar features should pay for themselves in ten years. I'll buy that!

I'll show you how to install those patio-door replacement glazing panels in Chapter 7, when we look at all possible window options.

6. Doors

Over the last three chapters we have taken a detailed look at the subject of heating a house. In Chapter 3 we decided to heat with wood, based on a projected post-retrofit bill of $470 for 5 cords of wood. In Chapter 4 we paused to look at oil and gas furnaces and boilers, and the marvelous improvements we could have made if one of those had been our heating choice. Finally, we investigated the possibility of displacing some of our "store-bought" fuel with free passive solar heat, and we found that we could reduce our fuel bill by a further 28 percent by incorporating simple and low-cost solar modifications.

Throughout, we've been using the heating load that was projected by our energy audit as the basis for calculating our savings. Now that we know what 100,000 Btu of wood heat will cost, we're ready to make some decisions about that thermal envelope. And we'll start with those small but most obvious and important components — the doors.

INTRODUCTION

First, let's refresh our memories about thermal envelopes. You'll recall from Chapter 2 that the thermal envelope is defined as the complete collection of surfaces which serve as a barrier to heat flow between the inside living space and the outside (see Illustration 2.11). Doors are obviously such pieces in the thermal envelope. Not so obvious are doors that are more familiar by other names: attic scuttle, attic access panel, trapdoor, and basement bulkhead are a few of their aliases. As we tour the house, I find that I have four doors: front entrance, kitchen entrance, basement bulkhead, and attic scuttle.

THE THERMAL ENVELOPE

An additional door now leads to the old woodshed. But since the shed is scheduled for removal, I'll simply board up and insulate the doorway. Each of these doors has equal importance in terms of potential heat loss per square foot. Because their uses differ, however, their retrofit solutions may also prove different.

FUNCTIONS OF DOORS

You may think that the only function of a door is to let building occupants come and go. Not so! Wouldn't you be very unhappy if your door didn't also:

6.1

• **Welcome your friends** (Illustration 6.1). Just as a dog says a lot about its master by the way it behaves, a door says a lot about the people who live behind it by the way it looks. It can be welcoming, forbidding, or boring! My favorite door is located on a solid slate-gray house (gray clapboards, gray trim, gray roof). This door is purple as a grape. I know the people behind that purple door; an outwardly sober, conservative appearance is betrayed by their mischievous front door.

6.2

• **Keep intruders out** (Illustration 6.2). Not all people who come to your door are friendly. No door will keep a really determined intruder out (in the North Woods they'll just chain-saw a hole through your living-room wall), but your door should at least slow them down.

6.3

• **Admit large objects** (Illustration 6.3). If you have a choice about the size of a door, grab a Sears, Roebuck catalogue (the architects' bible). It lists the dimensions of nearly everything you might ever want in your house!

6.4

• **Take abuse** (Illustration 6.4). The way we treat doors is shameful. Abuse from frustrated occupants, thrown objects, and amusement rides for children — these are just a few of the stresses in the life of a door. When you consider that most doors are constructed like your finest furniture, it's surprising that they last as long as they do.

6.5

• **Let breezes in** (Illustration 6.5). We most often consider windows for ventilation. But the standard exterior door, with an opening of 20 square feet, admits as much air as four double-hung windows. Since the door has to open for other reasons anyway, consider the lower-cost ventilation option of fixed windows plus screen doors.

6.6

• **Keep out wind, rain, and snow** (Illustration 6.6). When we're not ventilating, chances are we're battening down the hatches! We ask the same door that admits cool evening breezes in the summer to stop the Montreal Express during the winter.

To understand how a door performs all of these contradictory functions, let's take a closer look at the way doors are constructed. Later in this chapter I'll show you how to make a door that is probably superior in most ways to your present door. But for the moment, let's look at a conventional door.

Illustration 6.7 shows a paneled entrance door. As a door its performance is dubious; but as a piece of cabinetry it is superb. Recognizing (or experiencing) the propensity of wood to swell and shrink across, but not along, the direction of grain in response to the varying seasonal moisture content of the atmosphere, manufacturers construct the panel door basically of four lengthwise perimeter members. These pieces are doweled and glued together. Since some 80 percent of the door's dimensions is defined by these members, the potential for swelling is reduced correspondingly. The 20 percent that remains is troublesome, however, since the door shrinks in winter precisely when we would like it to fit the tightest.

HOW DO DOORS WORK?

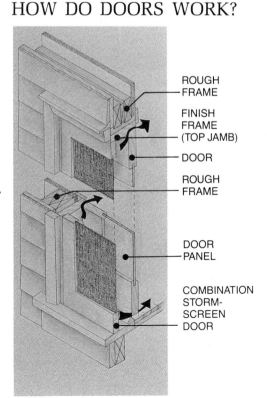

ROUGH FRAME

FINISH FRAME (TOP JAMB)

DOOR

ROUGH FRAME

DOOR PANEL

COMBINATION STORM-SCREEN DOOR

Insertion of the tongue-and-groove panels into this basic structural framework accomplishes several purposes: the door is lighter in weight; the door is more decorative; and the panels and frame can swell and shrink independently.

The door is fitted precisely into a door frame consisting of top jamb, side jambs, and threshold. The three jambs are dadoed or grooved on both indoor and outdoor faces to receive both the inside door and an outside storm door (the middle of the jamb serves as a door stop for both doors).

Providing for an outside combination storm-screen door in this way makes weatherproofing less effective. The inner door must open inward, making a watertight threshold impossible. And since the door latch is the single point resisting an inward thrust, burglar-proofing is also made more difficult.

There are two significant stages of carpentry in building a house: framing and finish. Framing involves assembling the structural frame, using materials of large dimension and working to a nominal accuracy of $\pm$ 1/4″. Finish carpentry involves carefully fitting, to an accuracy of 1/16″, those pieces which will be visible and those which comprise the openable parts of the envelope. The door and door frame (often purchased together as a "prehung" unit) are part of the finish, and are shimmed and nailed into a rough opening in the frame. In this way, the door and its frame bear none of the loads imposed on the house frame.

WHAT'S WRONG WITH CONVENTIONAL DOORS?

First, they are too expensive (everything about a house is too expensive!). Mainly, however, the major problems with old-fashioned doors are related to energy loss.

Doors were the bane of my existence until I discovered how to make my own. I've already mentioned the seasonal swelling and shrinking that occurs every six months in synch with Nature. Just as every winter my front door shrank, every summer it would swell and stuck. I finally became so angry that I took the door off its hinges and planed it down. The first two planings proved insufficient and so, after hinging and unhinging the door twice, I reached for my circular saw (the one with the big ugly teeth that go around in a circle at 527,000 rpm). This impulsive act demonstrates why I primarily write about, rather than practice, carpentry. In thirty seconds I solved the sticking problem for eternity. The only problem is that now I can tell who is on the other side of the door from the color of his or her shoes!

The second problem is caused by those elegant little panels. At their thickest point they measure 3/8"; at the edges a feathery 1/8". Even though wood is a better insulator than stone, the overall R value of the panel door is only slightly better than that of a double-glazed window.

Finally, except for the very oldest and the very latest doors, door manufacturers haven't taken weatherstripping seriously. Back when carpenters were craftsmen, interlocking weatherstrips were common; today we have steel doors and magnetic strips. But for forty years the only door in the house with a decent weatherstrip was the one on the refrigerator!

DOOR RETROFIT OPTIONS

We earlier identified three types of doors in this house: the entrance, the basement bulkhead, and the attic scuttle. All of these doors need retrofitting but, because I'll use them for different purposes, my options will vary. Let's take one door at a time.

Entrance Doors.   Option One would be to repair the existing doors: remove, strip the paint, reglue and reinforce, relocate the hinges, install new locks, repaint, and weatherstrip. The resulting doors would still have their original low R values of 2.2; addition of quality storm doors would be appropriate.

Option Two would be to install new *insulated doors*. These are steel-clad doors with wood frames, insulating foam cores, and magnetic weatherstrips—excellent doors that solve all of the above-mentioned problems when installed in a new house. Sounds like a great option? Unfortunately, there is one very large problem with their use in an older home. Because they are steel-clad, they cannot be trimmed to fit into an existing door frame, but must be used with their own prehung frames. In retrofitting this means removing and replacing *all* components associated with the previous door: door, door frame, threshold, interior and exterior trim—an expensive operation!

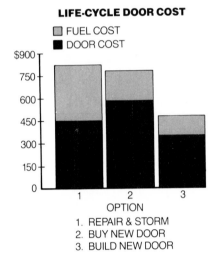

LIFE-CYCLE DOOR COST

- ▨ FUEL COST
- ■ DOOR COST

OPTION
1. REPAIR & STORM
2. BUY NEW DOOR
3. BUILD NEW DOOR

6.8

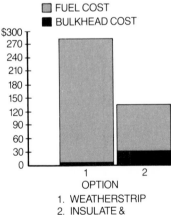

LIFE-CYCLE BULKHEAD COST

- ▨ FUEL COST
- ■ BULKHEAD COST

OPTION
1. WEATHERSTRIP
2. INSULATE & WEATHERSTRIP

6.9

Option Three would be to build our own insulated doors to fit the existing door frames. We can beat modern door manufacturers by constructing a foam-filled door, substituting plywood for steel, but cut to fit the old frame exactly—a low-cost option.

Illustration 6.8 shows the life-cycle costs of my three options. Repairing the two existing doors is surprisingly expensive because of the great amount of labor involved. The resulting low R value (R 3.2) also adds a high lifetime fuel penalty. The cost of fuel is low for factory-built thermal replacement doors, but the cost of rebuilding the frames leads to high initial cost. The homemade doors have both the lowest initial cost and lowest lifetime fuel cost. So, provided I dare to tackle the job myself, that's the route I'll take.

Basement Bulkhead. There's nothing very exotic about a bulkhead door. Most people use them twice a year to pass objects into and out of basements. If I handle mine gently, I can probably nurse the present door through the next thirty years (only sixty openings)! The interior vertical door is constructed of 3/4″ tongue-and-groove boards. At ground level is an exterior sloping door of similar construction. Overall, the R value is about 3. Option One, the cheapest way to go, is to do nothing but weatherstrip the existing interior door for only $3.

Option Two is to fasten slabs of 1½″ rigid foam insulation to the outside face of a 3/4″ piece of plywood (the outside face because fire codes require foam insulations to be protected by a material having a 15-minute fire rating on the living-space side). This option will cost about $30, including weatherstripping.

Illustration 6.9 shows that, at such small cost, the thirty-year fuel-cost projection swings my decision. I'll spend $30 on a new insulated bulkhead.

Attic Scuttle. Last, but not least, is that little door in the sky, the attic scuttle hole. Some folks have scuttles, others have attic doors, folding stairs, or no access at all. But those who do have a way into the attic should remember that an unheated attic is at essentially outdoor temperature, and a door leading to it should be treated as any other exterior door: it should be insulated and weatherstripped.

Option One is simply to weatherstrip the crummy old piece of gypsum drywall presently in place, at a cost of $1.

Option Two is to fasten a piece of that 1½″ rigid foam to the top side of the same drywall for the large sum of $5. Illustration 6.10 shows that, while we're not dealing with the federal budget, Option Two will leave me $44 richer in thirty years.

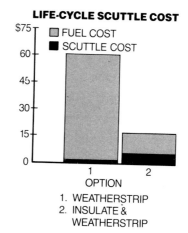

LIFE-CYCLE SCUTTLE COST

- FUEL COST
- SCUTTLE COST

OPTION
1. WEATHERSTRIP
2. INSULATE & WEATHERSTRIP

6.10

Illustration 6.11 shows how I built my own high-R, no-stick, no-warp door.

HOW TO BUILD AN INSULATED DOOR

STEP 1. Remove the existing door and all of its hardware. (Don't throw the hardware away, however, until you determine the replacement cost; the prices down at the hardware store will shock you!) Place the door on top of a sheet of 5/32″ Lauan plywood with the best plywood face up and carefully trace its outline onto the plywood. Repeat with a second piece of plywood, this time with best face down.

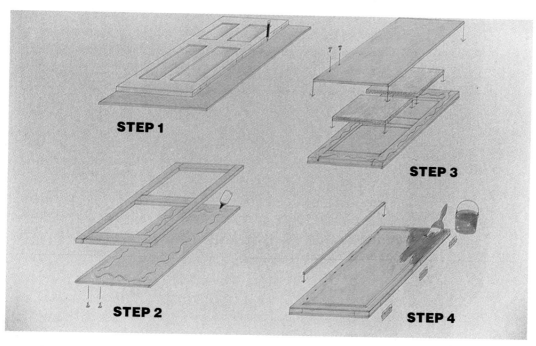

STEP 1

STEP 2

STEP 3

STEP 4

6.11

STEP 2. Cut two straight and dry 2 × 4s to the lengths of the two longer panel sides, plus three 2 × 4s to fit between at top, middle, and bottom. Carefully lay out the 2 × 4 pieces, using one of the plywood panels as a guide. Draw a line with a pencil, or snap a chalk line, one inch in from the perimeter of the panel, good side down. Apply waterproof glue, such as Resorcinal or epoxy glue, in a ribbon pattern along the pencil line. Fasten the 2 × 4s to the panel using 1¼″ drywall screws every 6 inches along the line. (A power screwdriver is just the thing here.) Note that your door will remain forever in the shape assembled at this point, so make sure the assembly is performed on a perfectly flat surface, such as the floor.

STEP 3. Cut rigid insulating foam to fill exactly the 1½″ thick voids between the 2 × 4s. Any type of foam will work. If you don't have 1½″ foam, use two sheets of 3/4″. Then apply glue to the faces of the 2 × 4s and screw the second panel, good side up, to the 2 × 4s around the perimeter. Allow the glue to set for twenty-four hours.

STEP 4. Try the new door in the old door frame. Since you used the original door for a pattern, the new door should fit perfectly. If not, plane or sand the offending edges until it does. Then glue and nail strips of "screen molding" over the drywall screws. Paint both faces and all edges with oil-base primer paint. After the primer dries, remove burrs and raised grain by rubbing with coarse steel wool, and apply two coats of grape-purple paint! Finally install hinges and locks, and the plastic tension strip weatherstrip material shown in Illustration 6.12.

Options. The drywall screws and screen molding may be omitted, provided sufficient pressure is applied during curing of the glue. One method is to pile about ten sheets of drywall or plywood on top of the door.

A second option is to remove the screws after curing and fill the voids with wood putty before painting. It all depends on how attractive you find the moldings.

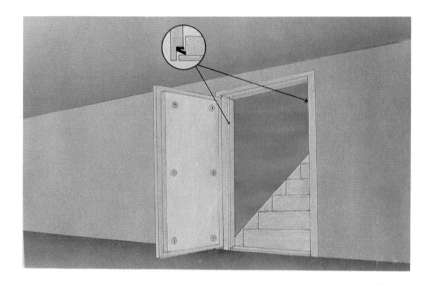

Illustration 6.12 shows how to replace an existing inner bulkhead door with a sturdy weatherstripped and insulated version.

HOW TO BUILD AN INSULATED BULKHEAD DOOR

STEP 1. Remove the existing door from its hinges and place it on top of a sheet of 3/4″ CDX plywood (it looks crummy, but it works superbly!). Trace the outline of the old door on the plywood and cut along the pencil lines.

STEP 2. Attach the new plywood door to the old hinges, which you've wisely left attached to the old door frame. Latch the door in the closed position, run around to the outside, and trace onto the plywood the line where the door stop meets the plywood.

STEP 3. Cut a piece (or pieces) of rigid foam to fit about 1/4″ inside the pencil lines. Fasten the foam to the outdoor side of the plywood with roofing nails or screws and washers. The door should now close as before but the rigid foam will fill the door stop space.

STEP 4. Apply self-adhesive strips of plastic tension strip weatherstrip to the inside face of the door stop. The opening of the V should face outdoors. If the surface of the door stop is too rough or dirty for good adhesion, the weatherstrip can be applied to the plywood face instead.

HOW TO BUILD AN INSULATED ATTIC SCUTTLE

Illustration 6.13 shows how to insulate and weatherstrip an overhead attic access panel or scuttle.

STEP 1. Build a plywood dam around the opening, high enough to contain any possible future thickness of attic insulation. Unless you are on Baffin Island I feel confident in recommending a height of 16″ to 18″. The plywood pieces may be simply screwed to the present finish, or the old finish removed and the plywood screwed to the framing of the opening.

STEP 2. Cut a piece of plywood or gypsum drywall 1/4″ smaller than the opening in both dimensions. Attach one or more pieces of rigid foam (any type) of the same dimensions to the plywood with long screws and washers, or to gypsum drywall with a building mastic recommended by the foam manufacturer.

STEP 3. Apply self-adhesive strips of soft foam (either open-cell or closed-cell) to the perimeter of the panel face.

STEP 4. Trim the ceiling opening with a molding of your choice, but inset enough to cover the foam weatherstrip from view. In case you are wondering, soft foam is recommended here rather than tension strip because the light weight of the panel is insufficient to effect a good seal.

Other Attic Doors. Vertical attic doors should be treated in the same way as basement bulkhead doors. Attic folding stairs require construction of an insulation dam similar to that in Illustration 6.13 plus an insulated panel hinged to and closing against the top edge of the dam.

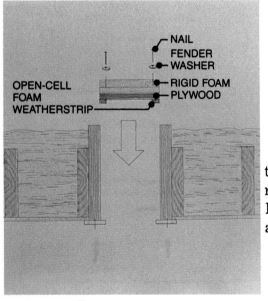

OPEN-CELL FOAM WEATHERSTRIP
NAIL
FENDER WASHER
RIGID FOAM
PLYWOOD

6.13

7. *Windows*

In the last chapter we found cost-effective, energy-saving solutions for our old, timeworn doors—the first set of thermal envelope surfaces we've tackled. Doors present a challenge because they serve many other functions in addition to stopping heat flow.

In this chapter we turn our attention to windows. Of all the surfaces of the thermal envelope, only windows offer the possibility of actually lowering our heating and cooling bills. In Chapter 5 we saw that the winter solar gain through windows could exceed their heat loss and thus reduce the need for fuel. And in Chapter 8 we will see that, properly shaded or insulated, windows can act as a valve in a natural cooling system to lower summer cooling costs.

Windows serve more functions than doors. It is not surprising, therefore, that they are physically more complicated and present a greater challenge. I prefer to think of them, however, as greater opportunities for energy savings.

FUNCTIONS OF WINDOWS

The origin of the word *window*—"wind-eye"—indicates its primary uses: to admit the wind, and to let people see outdoors. Over the years, many other functions have developed. Here is my list of the six most important functions of windows.

7.1

• **Permit us to see outside** (Illustration 7.1). When I was much, much younger, I worked for several years in a windowless underground laboratory. Even though everyone in the lab was young and male, the primary topic of conversation was neither sex and drugs nor rock-and-roll; it was the weather! It stands to reason that man could not have spent over 500,000 years roaming free and then suddenly be happy in a windowless, fluorescent-lit box.

7.2

• **Keep strange people from seeing inside** (Illustration 7.2). I don't mean strangers; I mean strange people! Because of the reflectivity of window glass and the great difference in ambient light levels between inside and outside, daytime visual privacy is not a problem. At night, however, the relative light intensities reverse, and, without window coverings, we're all on exhibition.

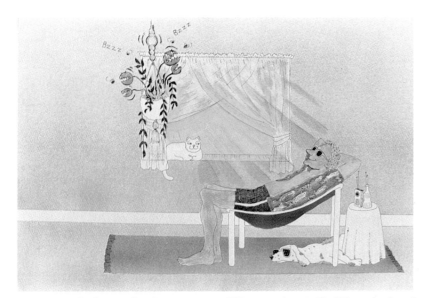

7.3

• **Let in light and solar energy** (Illustration 7.3). Man evolved under natural daylight and so it's not surprising that his eyes function best with that source. Since sunlight also is free, windows will always remain our best lighting source.

7.4

• **Keep out wind, snow, and rain** (Illustration 7.4). Obviously we want windows, like all of the other thermal envelope surfaces, to exclude the harsher elements. Because windows are ordinarily openable, that proves tricky. Even if the window is nonoperable, keeping rain out of the window construction itself (and causing deterioration) requires careful attention.

7.5

• **Let in the breeze, but keep out the bugs** (Illustration 7.5). Atmospheric motion in winter is called "wind"; in summer it's called a "breeze." However, some of the less desirable summer fauna must be prevented from entering with the breeze.

7.6

• **Keep intruders out** (Illustration 7.6). This is a primary function of doors as well. Burglars will try to gain entry through doors first, but, failing that, will next try the windows, especially those near the ground.

Transmission of light (Illustration 7.7). Ordinary window glass transmits, or passes through, about 87 percent of the total solar radiation striking it head-on (incident angle of 0°). The remaining 13 percent is either reflected back to the atmosphere or absorbed within the glass and converted to heat. As the direction of radiation changes from perpendicular to a more glancing angle, the percentage reflected increases; rather slowly at first (15 percent at 45° and 21 percent at 60°) and then abruptly (100 percent at 90°). Since the intensity of solar radiation is greatest head-on, we can say that a layer of glass transmits approximately 87 percent of the solar radiation striking it.

A second layer of glass would transmit 87 percent of the radiation received on its surface, as well. Therefore, the transmission through double glazing would be .87 × .87 = .76; and the transmission through triple glazing would be .87 × .87 × .87 = .66.

The transmission of sunlight through glass can be increased in two ways: (1) by decreasing the absorption due to iron impurity content; and (2) by decreasing the reflectivity of its surface with an antireflective coating.

The extra cost of these treatments has resulted in their use only in active solar collectors. New to the market are plastic films with extraordinarily high transmissions. These films can

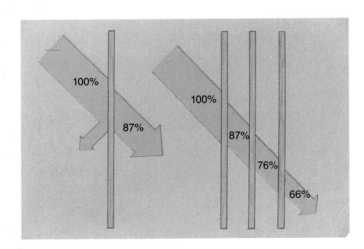

7.7

be placed inside factory-sealed double glazings, where they dramatically decrease heat loss without noticeably decreasing light transmission. Unfortunately, in considering this kind of treatment for my house, I have not found the price to be in a competitive range.

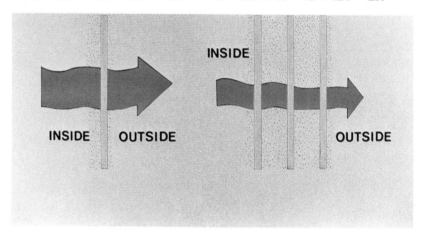

$$R = .68 + .01 + .21 = 0.9 \qquad R = .68 + .9 + .9 + .21 = 2.7$$

INSIDE

INSIDE   OUTSIDE

OUTSIDE

7.8

Transmission of heat (Illustration 7.8). This brings us to the second sort of transmission through windows — that of heat. The ideal window would transmit all light, but no heat. Illustration 7.8 shows how a window retards heat flow. The R value of a single glazed window is about 0.9. Although small, this value is actually the *total* of several smaller R values added together: the R value of an inside layer of air trapped by friction against the glass (0.68); the glass itself (.01); and a similar outside layer of air (0.21). Of all three, the R value of the glass material itself is the smallest! Upon reflection (no pun intended), this seems reasonable, since the 1/8″ thickness of the glass is only about 1/100 of a foot, and the R value of stone, a comparable material, is 1.0/foot. Knowing that the R value of the glazing material itself is inconsequential, you can raise a knowledgeable eyebrow the next time a hardware clerk informs you that a 1/8″ thick plastic window is far superior to a glass window because of the R factor of the plastic!

When we add a second glazing, we add not only the glass itself, but its accompanying inside and outside layers of air. Therefore, we add another 0.9 to the total R value. As Illustration 7.8 shows, this process continues *ad infinitum*, adding 0.9 to the total R value with each layer of air and glass. Since the R value is a measure of resistance to heat flow, doubling the R value halves the heat flow. The three layers of glass shown lose one-third as much heat as a single layer.

How many window layers are cost-effective? That question requires a detailed analysis, involving the cost per added glazing, the local availability of winter solar radiation, the cost per Btu of heat for the fuel chosen, and the severity of the climate. Let's consider the incremental savings we can gain by adding more panes of glass—a classic example of the Law of Diminishing Returns. If the heat loss of a single-glazed window is defined as 1.0, then the incremental savings of successive layers are:

$$2\text{nd layer} = 1 \quad - \; 1/2 = 1/2$$
$$3\text{rd layer} = 1/2 - 1/3 = 1/6$$
$$4\text{th layer} = 1/3 - 1/4 = 1/12$$

Again, how many layers of window are cost-effective? Obviously, the answer to our question is likely to be "not many."

Net gain. Overall, do windows gain or lose more heat during the heating season? The net winter heat gain of a window is defined as the solar gain less the heat loss. Average winter solar gain varies by about a factor of 2 throughout the United States; the Northwest coastal region having the least, and the sunny Southwest the most. Winter heat loss is a function of the average difference between inside and outside temperatures, expressed as heating degree days.

Illustration 7.9 combines solar gain and heat loss for both single- and double-glazed windows facing four points of the compass in Portland, Maine. It is important to note that, because of its mild coastal climate, Portland's solar gain and heat loss figures are very typical of the northern half of the

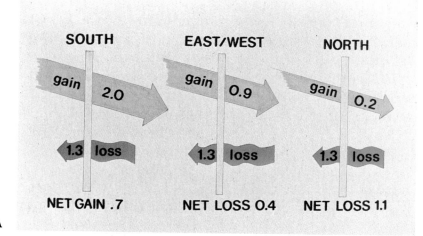

SOUTH   EAST/WEST   NORTH

gain 2.0   gain 0.9   gain 0.2

1.3 loss   1.3 loss   1.3 loss

NET GAIN .7   NET LOSS 0.4   NET LOSS 1.1

7.9A

country. The illustration shows that all but south-facing single-glazed windows are net heat losers. By adding a second glazing, we convert east-west windows to net gainers, even though solar gain is reduced by approximately 10 percent.

Can we determine the benefit of adding a third glazing? Let's consider south-facing windows first. A third glazing would reduce solar gain by about 10 percent, to 1.6 (100,000 Btu/sq.ft./yr.); but, recalling the Law of Diminishing Returns, we

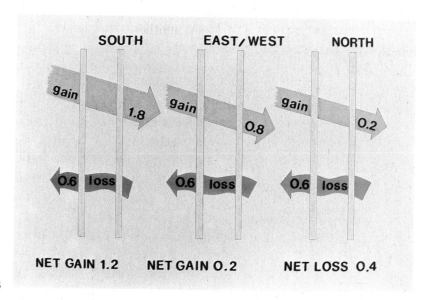

SOUTH   EAST/WEST   NORTH

gain 1.8   gain 0.8   gain 0.2

0.6 loss   0.6 loss   0.6 loss

NET GAIN 1.2   NET GAIN 0.2   NET LOSS 0.4

7.9B

find it would cut heat loss to only one-third of 1.3, or 0.4. Thus the *net gain* would remain at $1.6 - 0.4 = 1.2$; identical to that of the double glazing!

Because the solar gain is so much smaller in all other orientations, however, a third glazing would result in an improved net gain for all directions but south.

There you have the final answer to our question regarding the optimum number of glazings: it all depends!

WINDOW TYPES

Windows are categorized chiefly by the ways they open and close. Illustration 7.10 depicts the six most common types: fixed, awning, hopper, double-hung, sliding, and casement.

• **Fixed.** Although admitting ventilating breezes is an important function of windows, it is not usually necessary for all windows in a building to open. The more well-insulated the house, the less the need to open windows. In fact, by opening the windows of a well-insulated house on a hot day, you'll most often be admitting hot air. The price of a window can be accounted for by four roughly equal factors: glass, frame, operating gizmos, and advertising. If you eliminate the opening function, the price drops by one-quarter; eliminate the fancy store-bought frame and it drops another one-quarter, and what's left is not worth advertising. I'll show you at the end of this chapter how to install a special kind of fixed glazing—a factory-sealed patio-door replacement glazing—at one-quarter the cost of its operable equivalent.

• **Awning.** Its name is derived from the manner in which it opens—hinged at the top. This method of hinging allows air to enter but rain to be shed. Being short and wide, it's very often used in basement walls and bathrooms.

• **Hopper.** The hopper window is the mirror image of the awning, being hinged at the bottom. In fact, one popular (and very low-cost) brand of basement window is reversible between awning and hopper. Although the hopper looks like a rain collector, it most often opens inward, so any rain hitting the glass would run to the outside.

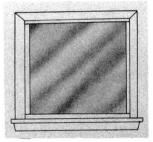

Fixed

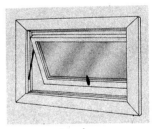

Awning

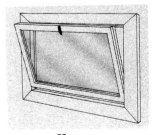

Hopper

7.10

Double-hung

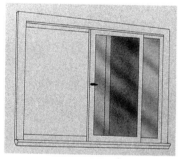

Sliding

Casement

7.10

• **Double-hung.** The generic window with which typical houses are built. Both upper and lower sashes slide vertically in tracks. Its advantages include a classic appearance ("windowness"), and the ability to ventilate at both the top and bottom on an outside wall simultaneously. A decided disadvantage, however, is the great length of air-leaking cracks — exceeded only by the horizontal glass slats of the jalousie window. We'll investigate the anatomy of the double-hung window in greater detail below.

• **Sliding.** The sliding, or gliding, window is essentially a double-hung window turned on its side. Two advantages are thereby gained: the open slider doesn't fight gravity and so requires no counterweights or springs; and one sash is often fixed, reducing the length of air-leaking cracks by nearly half. A giant version of the slider is the sliding glass or patio door. The patio door has become immensely popular because it solves two problems for one price: it admits large amounts of light, yet functions as a door. The simplicity of construction and operation makes the patio door-window a real construction bargain.

• **Casement.** The casement window resembles a glass door, swinging out from the side. Are you old enough to remember the little triangular side windows automobiles used to sport? Before the days when Detroit installed air conditioners in our automobiles without asking, these little air scoops delivered a terrific breeze in a moving automobile. The particular advantage of the casement window is its ability to do the same to a breeze moving past a stationary house. Almost every locale has a cooling breeze — a breeze that springs up in late afternoon or early evening. That breeze most often comes from one prevailing direction. Make sure your casement is hinged on the proper side to scoop the cooling breeze into your house.

Illustration 7.11 exposes the secrets and problems of that most common of all windows, the double-hung.

The window contains two sashes—rectangular frames formed of wood "rails"—into which fixed panes of glass are fitted. A sash may contain a single pane, or many panes separated by smaller wood members. Each sash slides vertically in its own track, formed either by grooved side jambs, or by jambs and stops. The "meeting rails" (upper rail of lower sash and lower rail of upper sash) come together in the closed position. The bottom rail of the bottom sash closes on the windowsill.

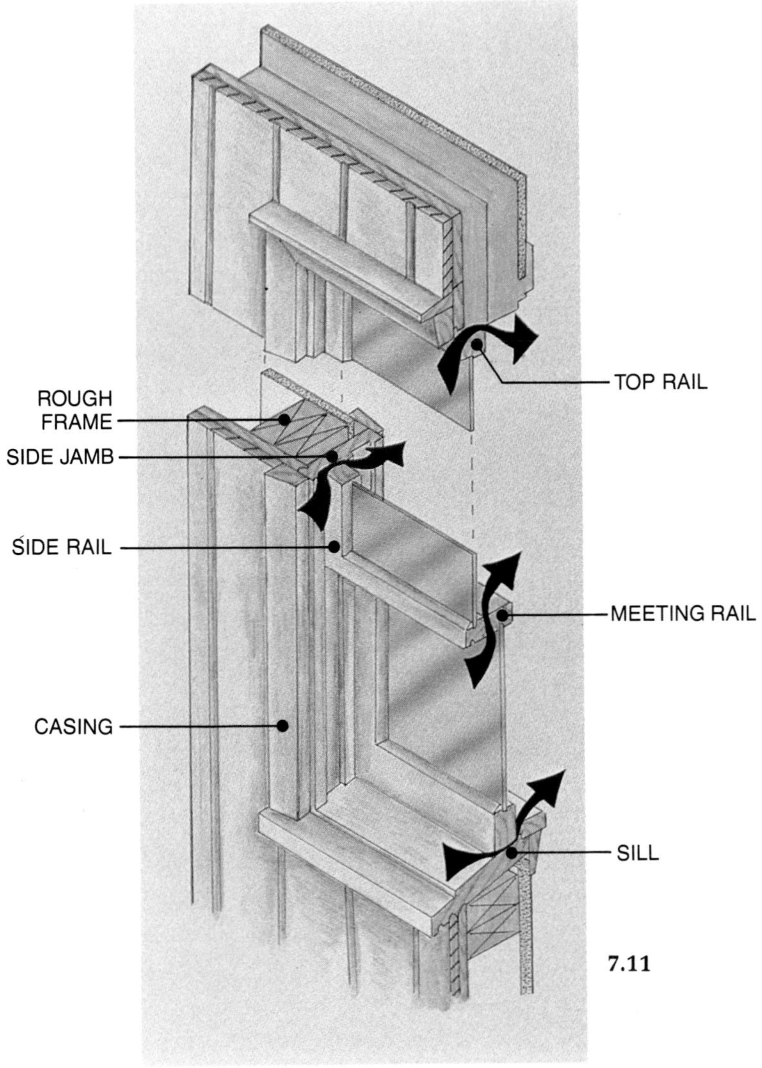

THE ANATOMY OF A DOUBLE-HUNG WINDOW

ROUGH FRAME

SIDE JAMB

SIDE RAIL

CASING

TOP RAIL

MEETING RAIL

SILL

7.11

The side and top jambs and the sill all together form the window frame, which is shimmed and nailed squarely into the rough opening of the building frame. As in the case of doors, the typical tolerance of the rough opening is ± 1/4″, while the tolerance for the moving parts of the window (window frame and sash) is ± 1/16″.

In order that the opened sashes not fall down under the influence of gravity, various mechanical schemes have been employed over the years. Some of my windows have spring-loaded pins which fit through the sash into holes in the side jambs. Others have pulleys and cast-iron counterbalancing sash weights rising and falling between side jamb and rough framing. The most modern versions use some form of spring within the side jamb.

We've now covered the anatomy of the double-hung window well enough to spot the potential trouble areas. Aside from the low R values of glazings in general, the major problem with these windows is infiltration. Air leaks through double-hung windows in three places:

- **Rails.** The arrows in Illustration 7.11 show the most obvious moving joints through which air commonly enters and departs. A 3′ × 5′ double-hung window has 19 linear feet of crack length, which must be weatherstripped.
- **Sash weight.** Provided the window has sash weights, the pulley holes in the side jambs are direct routes to the interior of the wall stud spaces. Being constructed only to 1/4″ tolerance, the stud space is usually a prolific source of outside air. In addition, this large space on either side of the window cannot be insulated and retain the intended function of housing the sash weights.
- **Finish.** Cracks invariably open in winter wherever two dissimilar materials meet, such as around the finish trim of windows. The solution is caulking.

Our old house has nine old single-glazed, double-hung windows that rattle audibly in their tracks. My neighbor, John Cole, says that I should save them because, at least, they slow down the wind! Restoring them *is* an option since the wood sashes and frames are still sound; they just seem to have grown apart like old friends.

Two of those windows are located in upstairs bedrooms that, typical of bedrooms, have only one door. The fire code requires two means of egress from each habitable room of a house and so the windows in those two bedrooms must remain openable. For the remaining seven windows, conversion to fixed glazing is a possibility.

The first energy conservation step for single-glazed windows is *always* addition of a second glazing. Since I'm interested only in permanent solutions, I can think of three options:

1. Replace the existing windows with new equivalent double-glazed, double-hung windows. Cost: $15.80 per square foot.
2. Repair, repaint, and weatherstrip the existing windows, then install good-quality outside combination windows. Cost: $8.36 per square foot.
3. Replace the existing windows with fixed, factory-sealed double glazing. Cost: $8.35 per square foot.

The last two options are very attractive in both cost and appearance because they don't require labor-intensive modification of the existing trim, either inside or outside.

Illustration 7.12 shows the life-cycle cost of the three options. Options 2 and 3 tie for first place, with a thirty-year life-cycle cost of $24/sq.ft. I'll repair the two upstairs bedroom egress windows and install new fixed glazing in the seven others. The reasons? First, I like new things; second, I don't like weatherstripping every few years; and third, as you'll see in the next chapter, I'm not going to need the ventilation.

OPTIONS FOR SINGLE-GLAZED WINDOWS

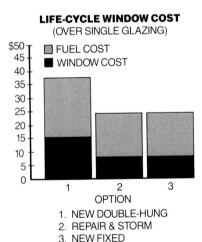

LIFE-CYCLE WINDOW COST
(OVER SINGLE GLAZING)

☐ FUEL COST
■ WINDOW COST

OPTION
1. NEW DOUBLE-HUNG
2. REPAIR & STORM
3. NEW FIXED

7.12

OPTIONS FOR DOUBLE-GLAZED WINDOWS

With the upgrading of the present single-glazed windows, all windows, including those in the new sunspace and those added to the south wall of the master bedroom, will be double-glazed. The next question is whether any further window treatment is justified. Further treatments fall into one of two categories:

1. An additional layer of glazing. In place 24 hours a day, an additional glazing reduces solar gain by 13 percent and conductive heat loss by 33 percent. How much it saves on infiltration depends on how tight the prime window is. In my case, very tight windows promise very small additional infiltration savings. Summer cooling savings are also slight.

2. Movable window insulation. Open eight to ten hours during the day and closed at night, MWI allows maximum solar gain but reduces night heat loss typically by 50 percent. Infiltration savings of MWI installed over my tight windows promises to be negligible. Since it is opaque, MWI can dramatically reduce the cooling load due to summer solar radiation.

So my options are:

• **Mylar inside storm.** One fascinating alternative is a heat-shrinkable Mylar plastic film. The film is attached to the face of the inside window trim with a clear double-sided self-adhesive tape and then shrunk with a hair dryer to a wrinkle-free, airtight membrane. Sales of this material have been phenomenal; my local hardware store had trouble keeping it on the shelf.

I'll have to admit to a moderate sense of excitement when I first saw the low price of this product. Fortunately, life-cycle cost analysis snapped me back to reality. The film is meant to be replaced *every* year! Including the estimated cost or value of labor, the film applied over tight double windows costs more than it saves. In fact, it proves to be more than twice as expensive as doing nothing at all!

• **Glass inside storm.** Inside storm windows consist either of a framed and weatherstripped pane of glass or plastic held against the window trim by a magnetic weatherstrip or set of tabs, or a pane of rigid plastic that snaps into a self-adhesive-backed plastic molding. In either case, the storm window ·is easily removed seasonally or in case of fire, and also has the potential of greatly reducing infiltration when installed over a leaky prime window. Glass has the disadvantage of being difficult to cut but the virtue of an almost unscratchable surface.

• **Acrylic inside storm.** Acrylic plastic panels have the advantage of ease of installation (cutting requires only scoring with a sharp knife and snapping) and the disadvantage of being easily scratched. Acrylic storms are essentially identical in price and thermal performance to glass. As I warned you above, claims of a higher-than-glass R value are sometimes greatly exaggerated.

• **Fancy wood shutter.** Insulating shutters typically fit inside the window frame and thus require expensive custom fabrication. Most shutters are attractively constructed of high-quality woods with foam cores. The price shown in the cost-analysis graph is half of what you might expect to pay for installed shutters, however, because of the dual heating and cooling savings.

• **Low-cost shutter.** There is one insulating shutter on the market packaged as a do-it-yourself kit. Its low price is due to its simple design and the use of common, low-cost building materials. This same low-cost shutter can be easily constructed by anyone with a modicum of carpentry skills, using materials available in lumber yards. More about this shutter below.

• **Roll-down shade.** Several versions of this MWI are available in a wide variety of decorative fabrics. In all MWIs the integrity of the air seal at bottom and sides is all-important. Cold dense air forms between the MWI and the window. If the MWI doesn't form a tight "pocket," the cold air will spill out, just like loose change out of your pants pockets when you stand on your head. Various versions use Velcro strips, sliding tracks, and magnets. I've used a cost of $3.08, roughly half of what you can expect to pay for the type of MWI installed, because of the dual role of MWI in saving on both heating and cooling costs.

• **Do nothing.** The final option is always to do nothing at all (I have to continually fight an inclination toward this option). After double-glazing and tightly weatherstripping, this option is actually a strong contender.

Decision

Illustration 7.13 shows the life-cycle cost of my window options. The assumptions include: (1) installation over airtight double glazing; (2) a life of twenty years; (3) wood heat at a cost of $.83/100,000 Btu; and (4) installed costs, less 15 percent federal tax credit.

The three inside storms turn out to cost more in my house than they would save. Keep in mind the assumptions, however. If they were installed in a house with more expensive fuel than wood and leakier prime windows, the inside storms could pay back quickly.

All three of the MWIs have lower life-cycle costs than any of the inside storms, as does the do-nothing option. But, because of its low installation cost, the low-cost shutter is the winner. Runner-up in my life-cycle cost contest is the shade with Velcro seals. My decision is to install some of both the low-cost shutters and the shades throughout the house.

I'm obviously convinced of the merits of movable window insulation. It pays back on the basis of conductive heat loss alone; the basis used in my calculations. Calculating the savings on any other basis is extremely difficult. Let me point out additional factors, however, which would make MWI pay back at least twice as fast:

• Comfort is determined by a combination of air temperature and the temperature of surrounding surfaces. By covering very cold glazed surfaces, MWI often raises the average comfort level of a room by several degrees. This permits lowering the thermostat by the same amount with attendant savings of 3–5 percent per degree. These savings typically *equal or exceed* the calculated conductive savings of MWI.

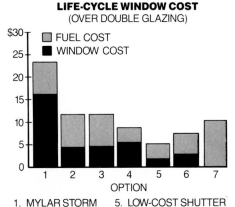

LIFE-CYCLE WINDOW COST
(OVER DOUBLE GLAZING)

☐ FUEL COST
■ WINDOW COST

OPTION

1. MYLAR STORM
2. GLASS STORM
3. ACRYLIC STORM
4. FANCY SHUTTER
5. LOW-COST SHUTTER
6. SHADE WITH VELCRO
7. DO NOTHING

7.13

- MWI is decorative and replaces conventional curtains and drapes at approximately the same price. Since we don't require draperies to pay back, why should we ascribe *any* cost at all to MWI?

HOW TO WEATHERSTRIP A WINDOW

Illustration 7.14 shows the various cracks in a double-hung window, which must be weatherstripped. Two types of motion occur between the movable sashes and the fixed frame:

- **Compression,** as top and bottom rails and frame come together in closing (cracks A and D).
- **Wiping,** as side rails and frames and the meeting rails slide past each other (cracks B and C).

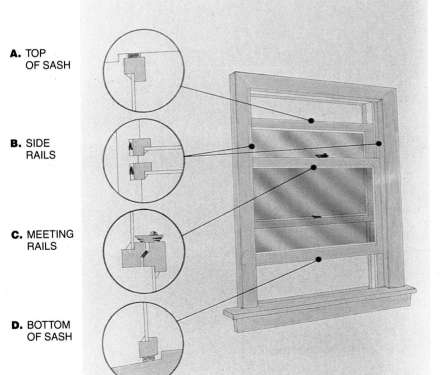

A. TOP OF SASH

B. SIDE RAILS

C. MEETING RAILS

D. BOTTOM OF SASH

7.14

The solution to compression is a compressible weatherstrip. Since a window is not opened as often as a refrigerator, a low-cost material will do. My recommendation is self-adhesive strips of soft foam.

The solution to wiping requires a tough, smooth weatherstrip which still retains the ability to fill a gap of varying width. Here my strong recommendation is strips of self-adhesive plastic-tension strip, with the opening of the V-shaped strip facing the outdoors. Consult Illustration 7.14 for the details.

HOW TO INSTALL FIXED DOUBLE GLAZING

First, of course, you have to purchase the glazing units. If you are adding, rather than replacing, a window, I strongly encourage you to install standard-size patio-door replacement units. Available in tempered glass (good in neighborhoods with children) and in standard sizes (28″ × 76″, 34″ × 76″, 46″ × 76″), they are a bargain. You should not have to pay more than $4/sq.ft. if you shop around at glass companies.

If you are replacing an existing window, your least expensive route is to retain the existing frame and finish and have the glazing unit custom-made. Have the glass company determine the dimensions! Custom units have little salvage value and cannot be sanded or planed down like a piece of wood. Expect to pay $6–$8/sq.ft.

Illustration 7.15 shows the replacement of a double-hung window with a fixed glazing.

> **STEP 1.** Remove the existing sashes. This requires removal of the outside window stop and the between-sash parting stop. If the window has sash weights, just cut the cord and have short-fiber fiberglass blown through the pulley holes by an insulation contractor.
>
> **STEP 2.** Apply strips of nonhardening "glazing tape" to the inside window stops all around. This beds the glass and prevents leakage of air and water.
>
> **STEP 3.** Place neoprene rubber setting blocks, 2″ to 3″ in length and a width equal to the thickness of the glazing unit, one-quarter of the distance in from each of the bottom

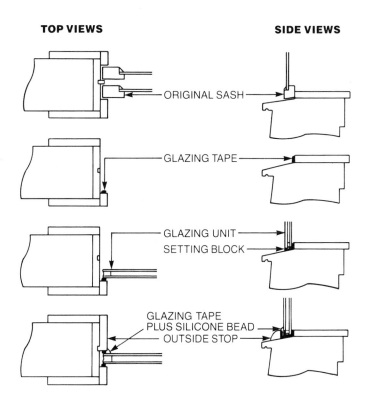

ORIGINAL SASH

GLAZING TAPE

GLAZING UNIT
SETTING BLOCK

GLAZING TAPE
PLUS SILICONE BEAD
OUTSIDE STOP

7.15

corners. The setting blocks support the entire weight of the glazing unit and prevent glass-breaking stress concentrations.

STEP 4. Apply strips of glazing tape to the edges of new outside window stops. Press the stops against the glazing and fasten in place with brass roundhead screws. Finally, run a bead of clear or white silicone caulk around the glass-stop joint; smooth with your finger. The silicone will prevent rain from penetrating the joint. Silicone can't be painted, so use white bathtub silicone if your house is white.

Illustration 7.16 shows how to build those low-cost shutters I rave about. I have to confess that my enthusiasm is partly due to my having conceived the design. The first one ever constructed is still saving heat with no signs of wear.

HOW TO BUILD LOW-COST INSULATING SHUTTERS

STEP 1. Measure the candidate window height (H), top width (W_T) and bottom width (W_B), measuring between the inside faces of the window jambs. Do this one window at a time. You may think you have ten identical windows but you'll be sorry if you act on that assumption!

STEP 2. Subtract 3/8″ from each H, W_T, and W_B. An accuracy of 1/16″ is preferred, but 1/8″ will do. If you have trouble with the fractions, consult a high school student.

STEP 3. Cut the face panels of Thermoply, a tough 1/8″ sheet of cardboard with foil faces, used in construction as building sheathing. The material is available in either kit form from MWI dealers or as 4′ × 8′ sheets at lumberyards, and comes in two versions: foil-foil faces or foil and white plastic faces. The first two panels should be cut to the *new* (less 3/8″) H, W_T and W_B; the second two panels should be the same dimensions, less an additional 1/4″.

STEP 4. Cut 1″ × 2″ strapping (actual dimensions are 3/4″ × 1½″) to form frames equal in outside dimension to the larger panels. This wood can be of any species; but it must be dry, straight, and without large knots. If all other sources fail, buy square-edged pine molding at your lumberyard. The joints of the frames can be held together temporarily with staples.

STEP 5. Run continuous beads of white carpenter's glue around the perimeter of the larger panels, and place the panels on top of the wood frames.

STEP 6. Taking care to keep the panel edges and frame aligned, fasten the panels to the frames with carpentry staples at least 1/2″ long. Hammer staples flush, if necessary.

STEP 7. Cut decorative fabric 4″ wider and longer than the panel size and wrap around panel and frame. Staple fabric edges to back of frame, leaving an inch of exposed wood. Fold fabric neatly at corners.

STEP 8. Glue the smaller back panel to the frame. Use lots of books, etc. to apply pressure overnight while glue cures.

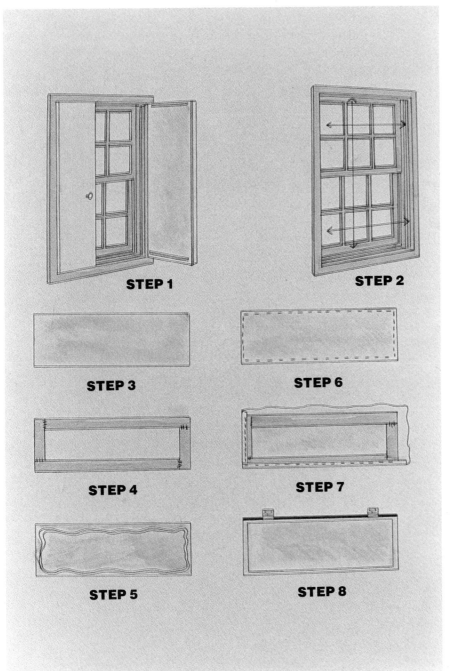

STEP 1

STEP 2

STEP 3

STEP 6

STEP 4

STEP 7

STEP 5

STEP 8

7.16

Make sure the shutter cures on a perfectly flat surface, such as the floor, as the shutter will eternally retain this shape.

STEP 9. Attach "loose-pin" hinges to the edges of one shutter (do not mortise or recess). Attach second set of hinges either to the edge of second shutter (regular shutters) or to the back (side facing window when closed) faces of both shutters (bifold shutters).

STEP 10. Supporting shutters on a scrap of Thermoply placed on the windowsill, install shutters along window jamb or inside edge of trim.

STEP 11. Apply self-adhesive foam weatherstrip to all vertical edges of shutter, and to the bottoms of the back faces. Install a 3/4" × 3/4" wood stop to meet the bottom foam strip on the windowsill. Finally install knobs to facilitate opening and closing.

8. Cooling

We covered the topic of winter heating in Chapters 3 through 5. But because of the large heating effect of summer solar radiation, we delayed our investigation of a cooling system until after considering the windows in our house. Now that we have chosen our windows, we can determine the extent of our cooling problem, and what we can do about it.

WHAT IS COOL?

First of all, what *is* cool? Cool, like warm, is a perception of *comfort*. The human body is analogous to a house. The metabolic system is our furnace, burning ingested fuel; and fat, skin, and hair constitute our thermal envelope. We too have a thermostat; it's set at 98.6°, however, rather than 68°.

The body maintains a remarkably constant internal temperature by balancing internal heat generation and the flow of energy between the body's surface and its surroundings. These energy flows are through the processes of:

- conduction (to air)
- convection (to air)
- evaporation (into air)
- radiation (to surrounding surfaces).

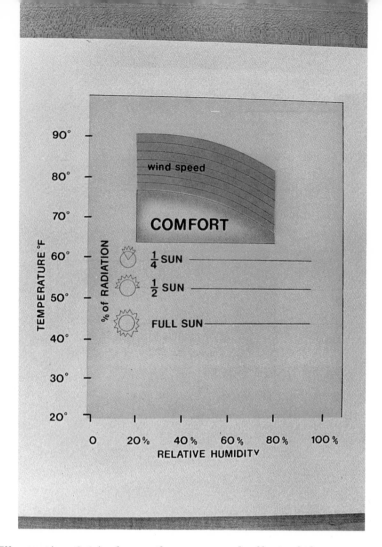

8.1A

Illustration 8.1A shows the measured effect of these energy flows on our perception of comfort. *Comfort* is technically defined as the feeling of being neither too warm nor too cool while performing sedentary tasks in ordinary indoor clothing. The majority of individuals tested reported feeling comfortable over a range of temperatures (vertical scale on left) and relative humidities (horizontal scale on bottom) within the flat-bottom egg-shaped "human comfort zone." The horizontal lines below the egg show how the increased bodily heat loss due to lower air temperatures can be compensated for by increasing levels of radiation. The radiation may come from the sun, or any other source measured in solar equivalents.

8.1B

In addition to solar radiation, internal heat generated by exercise can compensate for heat loss at low temperatures, and extend the lower limit even further. Marathon runners, internally producing 1,000 Btu per hour, can be quite comfortable at 32° clad only in skimpy clothing!

The curves above the egg show how higher air temperatures can be compensated for by air movement across the body. Air motion, or breeze, removes heat from the body in two ways: by convection and evaporation. Notice that the egg is curved at the top but flat at the bottom. The reason? When the body feels cool (near the bottom of the comfort zone) it doesn't sweat, and so cool comfort is independent of air humidity. At the top of the zone, however, the body is warm and sweats, and the rate of evaporation is very dependent on air humidity.

8.1C

8.1D

The comfort-zone chart thus shows that sedentary comfort can be achieved over a rather incredible range of conditions; from 45° in full sunlight and no wind to 85° in low humidity, total shade, and a strong breeze. There appears to be hope, then, that life *can* exist on earth without benefit of central air conditioning, provided we work with Nature's givens.

8.1E

We now know how a body becomes overheated, but what about its counterpart, the house it lives in? A house gains heat in much the same way (Illustration 8.2):

- By *conduction* of heat from warm outdoors to cooler interior through the surfaces of the thermal envelope.
- By *convection* or air leaks through the thermal envelope.
- By *solar radiation* through windows in the envelope. Solar radiation displaces the need for fuel heat in winter, but increases the need for cooling in summer.

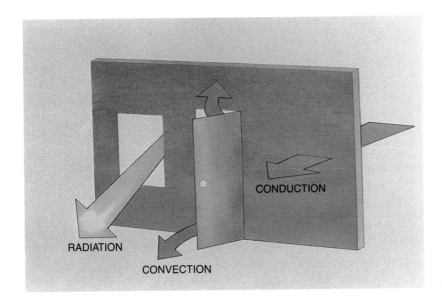

8.2

Of the three summer heat gains, which is most important? As usual the answer is, "It all depends." Conduction depends on outdoor air temperature and insulation levels of the building surfaces. The insulation that works to retard winter heat loss works just as well to retard summer heat gain. Convection depends on the airtightness of the envelope. The same caulking and weatherstripping that prevent winter loss of warm inside air also prevent summer gain of warm outside air. And solar gain depends on glazing areas, orientations, and degree of shading from the direct rays of the sun.

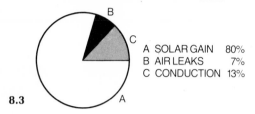

SUMMER BUILDING HEAT GAIN

A SOLAR GAIN 80%
B AIR LEAKS 7%
C CONDUCTION 13%

8.3

SUMMER WINDOW HEAT GAIN
(100,000 BTU/YR)

8.4

NORTH EAST SOUTH WEST
WINDOWS FACING

BLOCKING SOLAR RADIATION

Our retrofitted house provides an example of a typical well-insulated, weatherstripped house. Without taking any prior action to reduce summer solar gain, our annual heat-gain pie is distributed as shown in Illustration 8.3:

- 13 percent conduction through surfaces
- 7 percent infiltration through cracks
- 80 percent solar radiation through windows.

Looking at the pie, there is little question where we should focus our house-cooling attentions.

Illustration 8.4 breaks down our window solar gain by orientation:

- 10 percent from the north
- 20 percent from the east, due to some present shading by trees.
- 31 percent from the south, due to our added master bedroom glazing and the high summer sun angle.
- 39 percent through those new unshaded sunspace windows on the west.

In Chapter 5 we identified solar radiation as contributing a *useful* 28 percent of our winter heat gain, but here a *harmful* 80 percent of our summer heat gain. Permanently boarding up the windows would eliminate both, but isn't there some way to be selective and preserve the useful while eliminating the harmful?

The answer, to a remarkable extent, is yes. Illustration 8.5 shows eight different solar interventions:

- **Deciduous trees** are those which drop their leaves for the winter. The most effective trees are broad-leaved species, such as maples and oaks, that may block only 10 percent of the winter sun but as much as 90 percent of the summer sun. In addition, they provide a local summer air-cooling effect by evaporating or transpiring thousands of gallons of water into the atmosphere through their leaves. With apologies to Joyce Kilmer, "I think that I shall never see/an air conditioner lovely as a tree."

- **Vines** growing up a window trellis can provide the same sort of function. Perennial vines planted in the earth send out new leaves each year. Or you can plant an annual vine in a windowbox which will climb the trellis anew each year. An idea that intrigues me is planting my pole beans in windowboxes. They won't cast full shade until July in Maine, but by the first of August, I can open the window and pick my beans!

- **Reflective films** can be applied to the inside of a glazing to reject from as little as 10 percent to as much as 90 percent of the sun's rays. Films applied directly to glass are not good solutions for "solar" glazings, however, because they block winter radiation as well; and, once removed, they can't be reused.

- **Absorbing films** are even less desirable than reflective films, since the intercepted solar radiation turns to heat upon absorption. Much of the heat generated subsequently flows into the house, anyway.

- **Sunscreens** are typically mounted outside the glazing where they intercept a fraction of the incident sunlight. The blocked radiation is both reflected and absorbed but, since the screen stands away from the window, none of the absorbed heat passes through the glazing. Most screens can be removed in winter and reused the following summer.

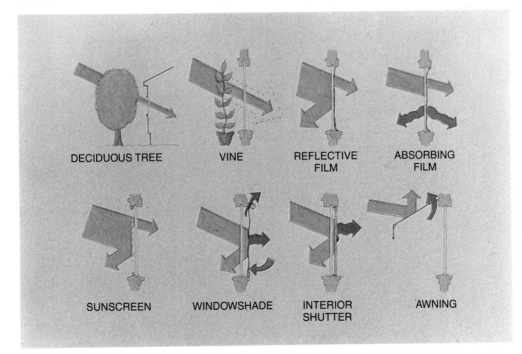

DECIDUOUS TREE   VINE   REFLECTIVE FILM   ABSORBING FILM

SUNSCREEN   WINDOWSHADE   INTERIOR SHUTTER   AWNING

• **Windowshades** can be effective or ineffective, depending upon their color and type of mounting. Very effective are light-colored versions of the tightly sealed movable window insulations noted in Chapter 7. On the other hand, the old-fashioned dark green roller-shade does virtually nothing to prevent solar gain, since the intercepted radiation is absorbed and turned into hot air inside the window.

• **Interior shutters,** if well designed, are the most effective sun stoppers of all. The foil-faced MWI shutters described in Chapter 7 not only reflect 90 percent of the radiation, but they insulate against conductive heat gain from the air as well. And like the MWI shades, they can be opened at night to admit cool air.

• **Awnings** of long-lasting synthetic fabric are now available. If they are removed in the winter, they should last the twenty years required to grow a shade tree. They should be long enough to shade windows fully until 4 P.M. on summer days. A slot at the top of the awning will prevent accumulation of hot air next to the window.

MECHANICAL COOLING AIDS

Our $197 summer heat-gain pie was cooked up assuming central electric air conditioning with a typical older equipment Coefficient of Performance (COP) of 6.5 and an electric rate of 6.8 cents/kwh. Actually, I've told a little white lie. The farmer who used to live in this house didn't have central air conditioning; he didn't even have a bedroom air conditioner. He probably just suffered in his sweaty sheets, sipping a concoction of ginger ale and molasses (a favorite of Maine farmers in haying season, I've been told). But I'll be damned if I'll put up with sleepless nights. I'm going to stay cool, and at minimum cost. I use the $197 figure only to show you how much I'll be saving with my better solution.

There are a number of mechanical means you can use to stay cool, other than electric air conditioners: window fans, whole-house fans, and furnace fans.

• **Window fan.** Provided the outside temperature is acceptably cooler than the house temperature, one or more window

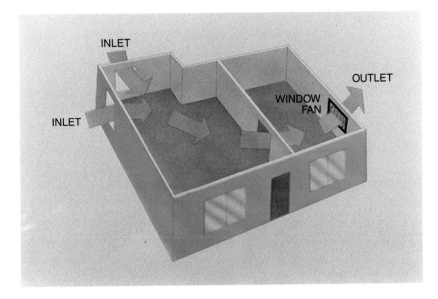

INLET

INLET

OUTLET

WINDOW
FAN

8.6

fans can provide inexpensive cooling. Illustration 8.6 shows that
the location of a window fan and the location of other open
windows and doors can precisely determine the areas cooled. In
the illustration, a single fan exhausting air from the living room
draws air in through bedroom windows at the opposite corner of
the house. With this arrangement, the coolest room will be the
bedroom; the next coolest, the living room (the moving air will
have picked up heat along the way); and the warmest rooms,
those out of the direct path of the moving air. This arrangement
is ideal for sleeping since the cooling benefit is concentrated
where it is most needed — and without the attendant noise of a
fan in the sleeper's ear. For most effective operation:

1. The fan should blow out, rather than in;
2. The fan should blow in the same direction as any
   prevailing natural breeze;
3. The window inlet areas should total at least twice the fan
   exit area.

Of course, windows in other rooms can be opened as well to
share in the cooling, but an average 20″ window fan can be
counted on to cool only about two rooms effectively.

• **Whole-house fan.** A whole-house fan (Illustration 8.7) is designed to cool the entire house. In areas with long hot summers, a whole-house fan should exhaust the entire volume of air in the house once per minute. In more temperate areas, such as the one I live in, an air exchange of once every two minutes is adequate. Whole-house fans are rated by their manufacturers for free-air delivery (no resistance to air flow, such as that caused by shutters and screens). In typical operation, most fans will deliver 70 to 80 percent of that figure. The volume of the house can be calculated as the sum of the volumes of all the rooms through which air moves (volume equals room floor area × ceiling height). For example, if I were to ventilate my entire house of 1,840 square feet at one air exchange per two minutes, I would need a fan that delivered:

$$\frac{1,840 \text{ sq.ft.} \times 8 \text{ ft.}}{2 \text{ min.}} = 7,360 \text{ cubic feet per minute (cfm)}$$

That translates into a free-air rating of about 10,000 cfm— an average figure for whole-house fans.

For either of the fans described, don't forget that the areas of the house to be cooled are determined by the location of the open windows and doors. For fine-tuning, the areas of the openings

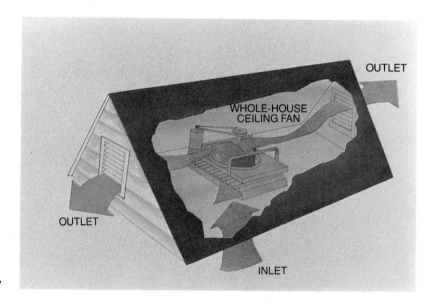

OUTLET

WHOLE-HOUSE
CEILING FAN

OUTLET

INLET

8.7

can be proportioned to the desired cooling effect. Again, the total intake area should be at least double the area of the fan opening.

• **Furnace fan.** If you have a warm-air furnace, you already have a built-in fan. Because moving air is perceived as cooler air, a furnace blower is typically sized to turn over house air only once every five to ten minutes. However, in a well-insulated house, this capacity should be sufficient to achieve the desired effect.

In this case, the desired effect is not an exchange of indoor and outdoor air, but an exchange of house and basement air. Basement air is likely to be cooler than upstairs air during a summer day for two reasons: (1) the large thermal mass of the basement masonry walls and floors acts like a massive flywheel to minimize daily temperature fluctuations; and (2) the much larger thermal mass of the earth surrounding the basement acts like an even larger flywheel to minimize yearly temperature fluctuations. Computer studies have shown that, with these masses acting together, an average basement can remove heat all summer long at the rate of a 3,000-Btu-per-hour air conditioner.

In order not to saturate the basement with house heat, however, we must be careful either to: (1) draw upon its capacity only on the hottest days; or (2) recharge its battery overnight with cooler outside air.

Ordinarily the furnace air distribution system is set up to circulate air only through the living space. In order to include the basement in the loop: (1) remove the furnace filter access panel, thereby short-circuiting the return air ducts; (2) open the door from house to basement to provide a path for the return air; and (3) switch the furnace blower control from "auto" to "on." Illustration 8.8 shows how the air would flow in my house — cool basement air is delivered through supply registers S and returns to the basement through a basement door and a large floor register R.

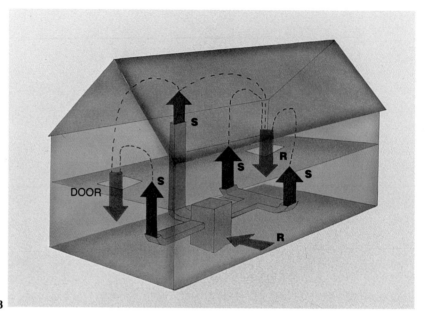

8.8

DOOR

A NATURAL COOLING AID

All of the above mechanical systems achieve cooling by using moving air. We found in Chapter 3 that we could heat our house by using natural air flow alone without resorting to any sort of fan. To what extent do you suppose we can use this effect for cooling the house?

The basic principle we used before was "warm air rises; cool air falls." And we found in Chapter 4 that the buoyancy of warm flue gases in a chimney was powerful enough to require a barometric damper in order to break the suction.

The same natural effect remains in force in the summer. If the air inside the thermal envelope is warmer than the air outside, the thermal envelope resembles a hot-air balloon. This bubble of warm air is restrained from rising into the atmosphere by the roof. If holes were opened at the top and bottom in the thermal envelope, the warm house air would rise out the top, to be replaced by inflowing cooler air near the ground.

In summer, we can take advantage of the "warm air rises" principle by installing openable skylights in the ceiling of the second floor. Opening the skylights and first-floor doors and/or windows will result in a cooling air exchange whenever the house air is warmer than outdoor air (Illustration 8.9).

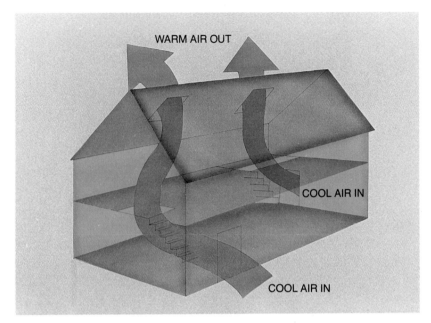

WARM AIR OUT

COOL AIR IN

COOL AIR IN

8.9

We have now seen ways to: (1) limit the amount of solar gain through our windows; (3) utilize thermal mass to absorb excess heat; and (3) ventilate a house through natural convection. Let's examine the practicality of utilizing all three tricks to cool our house naturally—without resorting to the expensive and unnatural use of a mechanical air conditioner.

I have used a computer to simulate the performance of my house on a hot summer day. The computer was given hourly values of outdoor air temperature and hourly solar radiation on each window, and uses the insulation R values, air exchange rate, and thermal mass of the house to predict the resulting indoor temperatures; they are shown in Illustration 8.10.

Curve A shows the outdoor temperature assumed by the computer, swinging from a low of 65° at 4 A.M. to a high of 95° at 4 P.M.

Curve B shows the resulting indoor temperature of the lightweight, poorly insulated, pre-retrofit house. The interior temperature rises rapidly due to conduction, infiltration, and solar gain to an oppressive 94° by suppertime. Sound familiar?

Curve C traces the temperature of the retrofitted house with closed foil-faced window shutters on all windows, and tightly

A NATURAL COOLING STRATEGY

TEMPERATURE SWINGS

—— OUTSIDE (A)   --- RETROFITTED (C)
······· PRESENT (B)   -·-· RETROFITTED
                          & PUMPED (D)

DEGREES F

100
90
80
70
60

6 AM   NOON   6 PM   MIDNIGHT

TIME

8.10

closed doors and windows. The resulting temperature now peaks at a considerably lower 83°. Note, however, that while the house gains heat slowly, it also loses it slowly during the night so that the temperature at 5 A.M. is still an uncomfortable 80°.

Curve D illustrates what I call "pumping." The principle is to make the house tight as a tick during the day (pump valve closed) but loose as a goose at night (pump valve open). More specifically, all doors, windows, and shutters are closed during the day and the thermal mass of the house has been increased by an additional layer of 1/2″ drywall on all walls and ceilings. As soon as the outdoor temperature falls below that of the inside, however, all apertures are thrown open, including three sky-lights in the upstairs ceiling. The result is an inside temperature that peaks at a reasonable 77° at 10 P.M., but that then follows the outdoor temperature down to a minimum of 67° by 5 A.M. Eureka! Passive cooling by active people—I love it!

"Yes," you say, "but you're in Maine." Disbelievers, please turn to Illustration 8.11 and 8.12, which show the average daily high and low temperatures throughout the United States during the month of August. You'll find that nearly the entire northern

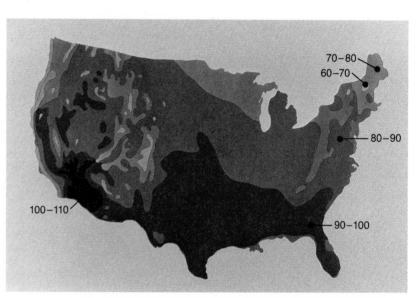

Mean Monthly Maximum Temperatures (August)

8.11

half of the nation qualifies for "pumping," having average overnight low temperatures below 65°. In addition, I haven't yet invoked the furnace blower–basement trick. If the outside temperature climbed even higher, or the overnight temperature failed to drop sufficiently, I could pull *all* the stops and pump basement air into the house.

Illustration 8.13 compares the life-cycle costs of three basic and diametrically opposed cooling options: (1) a new low-cost, medium efficiency (COP = 7.5) central air conditioner (CAC); (2) a new higher-cost, higher efficiency (COP = 10.2) air conditioner; and (3) my all-natural pumping technique. In the cost of pumping I've included the cost of the additional thermal mass layer of 1/2″ gypsum drywall on all walls and ceilings ($800), and half of the cost of the MWI shutters (the other half, or $800, is billed to winter heat savings). Those of you who insist on central air conditioning should note that the extra cost of the more efficient unit *was* justified by the twenty-year electric savings. But most impressive of all, I think, is the twenty-year fuel cost of natural cooling—nearly zero!

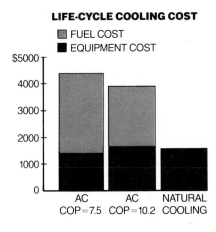

8.13

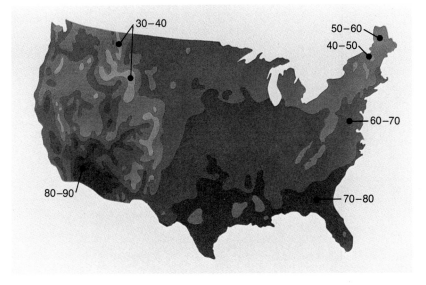

**Mean Monthly
Minimum Temperatures
(August)**

8.12

HOW TO PLANT A TREE

The farmer long ago planted a now mature row of maple trees along the property line just to the west of the house. As in the smile of a mature person, however, one of its members is now missing. Unfortunately the gap falls in line with my new sunspace, the glazing that accounts for 39 percent of my cooling load.

The short-term solution is closing the MWI on sunny days. A better long-term solution would be a shade tree. Long-term, I say, because a tree grown from seed requires about forty years to cast a respectable shadow.

Rich people can afford instant trees. They just order up a big tree from a "tree service" (that's where you look in the Yellow Pages) and, bingo, instant shade! But you don't have to be rich, I found. The farmer would smile down from heaven at what I discovered. There are an awful lot of unloved trees already growing in wrong places. I found a twenty-year-old sugar maple growing smack up against the barn. Left alone, it would ultimately damage the barn and have to be destroyed. Following the advice of my local agricultural extension agent, I moved the tree. Illustration 8.14 shows how.

STEP 1. Several months before moving day, cut the roots in a circle whose radius in feet equals the diameter of the trunk in inches. Use a backward spade to prevent lifting and tearing the roots. Immediately begin watering daily in order to make up for the loss of root area.

STEP 2. After the tree has dropped its fall foliage, remove about two-thirds of the small leaf-bearing branches by pruning. Dig a trench of depth equal to the radius of the root circle and undercut the remaining roots.

STEP 3. Tip the tree on its side and slip burlap under the root ball; tip to the opposite side and pull the burlap through. Tie the burlap up around the trunk to form a tightly wrapped root ball.

STEP 4. Transport the tree to its new location in a wheelbarrow or a pickup truck. Always lift the tree by the root ball, not by the trunk or branches.

STEP 5. Dig a hole 12″ wider and 6″ deeper than the root ball. Place 12″ of the loose soil back into the hole.

STEP 6. Place the tree in the hole (the root ball should now sit a few inches higher in its new home). Cut away most of the burlap from the top and sides. Refill the hole with the original soil. Mulch the ground surface with straw or bark chips. Drive three stakes equidistant around the tree and run wires to a common point above a large branch halfway up the tree. Thread the wires through short loops of old garden hose to protect the tree trunk. Continue watering until the ground freezes.

In twenty years, just when my MWI is falling apart, I should have a permanent solution!

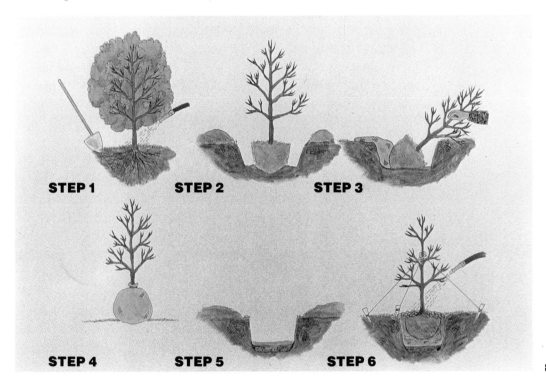

STEP 1   STEP 2   STEP 3

STEP 4   STEP 5   STEP 6   8.14

9. *The General Theory of Insulation*

INTRODUCTION

So far, we've determined exactly what each Btu will cost, and, from there, our annual heating and cooling costs. To do so, we've had to assume that the projection made by our energy audit was correct—that, indeed, we could create a thermal envelope as good as that specified by our auditor.

But there are a dozen different insulations. Which one should we use, and where, and how much should we install? These are questions *we* should be able to answer. If we don't understand how insulation works, our chances of creating an effective thermal envelope are slim.

This chapter is about insulation in general—how it works. The next chapter describes the details of installation.

FUNCTIONS
OF INSULATION

I pity insulation contractors. The poor contractor gets blamed for everything that goes wrong in a house. When the roof leaks, people assume the insulation in the attic is generating water spontaneously. When basement pipes freeze, insulation is blamed for heat deprivation. The worst instance I can remember was when I was asked to testify in court that, by insulating a wall, an insulation contractor had actually increased a home owner's fuel bill!

But it is reasonable to expect some things of insulation:

9.1

• **Stop winter heat loss** (Illustration 9.1). Insulation can't stop heat loss altogether; it can only slow it down. A house in winter is like a thermos bottle full of hot soup. Sooner or later, you're going to have cold soup. But the better insulated the jug, the longer you have hot soup.

9.2

• **Stop summer heat gain** (Illustration 9.2). A thermos bottle can also keep liquids cool in summer. The same with an insulated house. As we saw in Chapter 8, the temperature rise inside an insulated house on a hot summer day should actually lag behind the outdoor temperature rise.

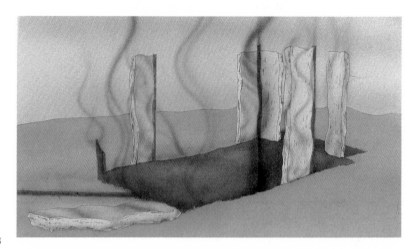

9.3

• **Be fireproof** (Illustration 9.3). Fireproof is a relative term. Almost nothing in nature is absolutely fireproof. Did you know that diamonds burn? It tickles me to think that they have exactly the same chemical composition as the charcoal that cooks my hamburgers. What we really should expect of insulation is that installing it in our home will not *increase* the risk or seriousness of fire.

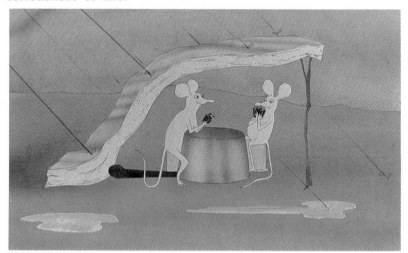

9.4

• **Be waterproof** (Illustration 9.4). This, too, is a relative term. You and I are not absolutely waterproof. After a number of years, even a piece of wood will sink in water. We should expect of insulation that moisture will not degrade its ability to retard heat flow when it is installed according to the manufacturer's directions.

9.5

• **Be vermin-proof** (Illustration 9.5). We hope that insulation will not be regarded by insect or animal as either delectable food or inviting shelter.

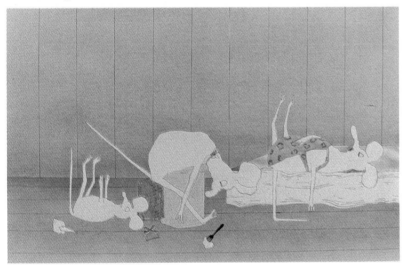

9.6

• **Be nontoxic** (Illustration 9.6). Again, a relative term. Burning or ingesting your vinyl shoes, dacron drapes, or urethane mattress may be harmful to your health, too. We just want our insulation to do its insulating job without indulging in chemical warfare.

Table 9.1

PROPERTIES OF HOME INSULATIONS

Form and type		R/IN.	Cost	Characteristics
Blanket and Batt				
Fiberglass (spun-glass fibers)		3.3	low	noncombustible except for facing; difficult with irregular framing
Rock wool (expanded slag)		3.3	low	noncombustible except for facing; difficult with irregular framing
Loose fill[1]				
Fiberglass (long-fiber)	attic	2.2	low	noncombustible
	wall	3.3	low	good in irregular spaces
Fiberglass (short-fiber)	attic	4.0	med.	noncombustible
	wall	4.0	med.	good in irregular spaces
Rock wool	attic	2.9	med.	noncombustible
	wall	3.3	med.	good in irregular spaces
Cellulose (paper fiber)	attic	3.7	low	combustible — specify "Class 1, noncorrosive"; can be damaged by water
	wall	3.3	low	
Perlite (glass beads)		3.3	high	noncombustible expensive
Vermiculite (expanded mica)		2.3	high	noncombustible expensive
Rigid foam boards[2]				
Molded polystyrene ("beadboard")		4.0	med.	combustible permeable — do not use below ground; max. temperature 165°
Extruded polystyrene ("Styrofoam")		5.2	high	combustible impermeable — best below ground; max. temperature 165°
Polyurethane/		6.2	high	combustible
Polyisocyanurate		7.0	high	good for walls and roofs outside; max. temperature 250°
Blown-in foam				
Urea formaldehyde		4.2	med.	presently banned; combustible; not damaged by water; may exude formaldehyde odor and shrink more than 3 percent if improperly applied

[1]All loose-fill insulation must be installed at manufacturer's recommended densities as shown on bag to ensure proper performance.

[2]All rigid foams are combustible and must be covered with 1/2″ gypsum drywall or equivalent 15-minute fire-rated material when used on interior.

Insulation is little more than a means of stopping air from moving. That's a fact! The thermal resistance, or R factor, of still air is about 4 per inch—a value exceeded only by the most expensive foam insulation products. The thermal resistance of the solid *material* of which an insulation product is formed is often 10 to 100 times less than that of the insulation product. So the manufacture of commercial insulation involves balancing the R-value–increasing effect of smaller air spaces against the R-value–decreasing effect of solid materials.

Illustration 9.7 shows the eight most common insulation products magnified. Clearly, 99 percent of the insulation you buy is air, and the solid material, whether in the form of strands or cell walls, is there merely to get in the way of the air.

Table 9.1 lists the most salient properties of home insulations: R value per inch of thickness, relative cost, and fire and moisture resistance.

• **Blankets and batts** are designed to fit between rafters, studs, and joists spaced the conventional 16″ or 24″ apart. Blankets come in rolls of various lengths; batts are usually four feet long. Both come in thicknesses of approximately 3½″, 6″, and 9″, and with a paper-and-foil facing or unfaced.

None of the products listed is permanently damaged by water, either in the form of condensation or running water. And, except for their facing, both fiberglass and rock wool are, for all intents, fireproof.

Their greatest advantage is low material cost. A very serious disadvantage for retrofitting, however, is the difficulty of completely filling the uneven framing spaces that characterize older homes.

HOW DIFFERENT TYPES OF INSULATION WORK

9.7A Long-fiber fiberglass

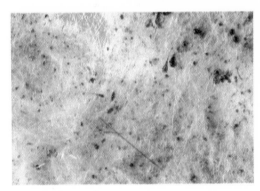

9.7B Rock wool

9.7C Short-fiber fiberglass

9.7D Cellulose

9.7E Vermiculite

• **Loose fills** are blown into cavities or over surfaces by special blowers. The blowing mechanism is designed to disperse the material uniformly at the manufacturer's recommended density.

The first two types listed—long-fiber fiberglass and short-fiber fiberglass—illustrate well the trade-off between material/air ratio and R value. The long-fiber version is that which we all have come to know and love. Installed under pressure in a wall cavity, its R value is typically 3.3 per inch; installed under no pressure in an open attic, the air spaces open up and the R value drops to only 2.2 per inch. Short-fiber fiberglass, because of its inherently smaller air spaces and fibers, achieves R 4 per inch in both wall and attic. More glass fibers are required to produce the smaller air spaces, so the short-fiber version is more expensive. But its higher R value and greater ability to fill small spaces is well worth the extra cost.

Rock wool is essentially the same as fiberglass, the only difference being the raw materials from which they are melted and spun: quartz for fiberglass, and iron-ore slag for rockwool.

Cellulose is shredded newsprint that has been treated with chemicals to be fire- and moisture-resistant. Since newsprint consists of the empty cells of wood fiber, the R value of cellulose is surprisingly high for such a low-cost material. Cost is an advantage, but potential corrosion of metals (due to the chemical additives) and irreversible loss of R value if it becomes thoroughly soaked are disadvantages.

Both perlite and vermiculite are absolutely noncombustible. A low R value and a high cost combine to result in an especially high cost per R. Used in small amounts, however, they are ideal for filling small voids between blankets and batts.

• **Rigid foam boards** are the thoroughbreds of insulation. With high cost and high R, they are appropriate wherever space is limited or conditions rule out the less expensive forms.

Molded polystyrene, or "beadboard," consists of a myriad of tiny styrene beads fused together under temperature and pressure to form a rigid slab. As Illustration 9.7 shows, each bead actually contains many cells, and tiny air passages remain between the fused-together beads. Water-vapor molecules (the gaseous form of water) travel readily through the air passages, making beadboard the only rigid foam that is not its own vapor barrier (see below). When beadboard is installed underground, liquid water slowly permeates the air passages, decreasing the overall R value.

Extruded polystyrene has approximately the same chemical formula as beadboard, but possesses quite different physical characteristics. Each cell is filled with a special gas of lower conductivity than air and shares single-thickness walls with its neighbors. Therefore there are no air passageways and the foam is impervious to water. Owing to a higher density and the geometry of its cell structure, extruded polystyrene is also extremely strong. It is the only type of insulation recommended for installation below ground.

Polyurethane and polyisocyanurate are chemically similar foams with a mixed open and closed cell structure. Initially filled with gas of extremely low conductivity, these forms have been advertised with "as manufactured R values" of up to 8.0 per inch. Because of the partially open cell structure, the gas slowly exchanges with air and the "aged R value" drops to the range of 6.2–7.0 per inch.

• **Blown-in foam.** Both urethane foam and polystyrene beads can be blown into cavities; they have the same physical properties as their rigid counterparts. One blown foam deserves special mention, however. Urea formaldehyde, now widely banned, was once one of the most popular retrofit products for wall cavities. Unfortunately, the success of the installation depended on temperature, the age of the chemicals, and the care taken by the installer. Shoddy quality control on the part of both manufacturers and installers resulted in many houses being permeated with lasting irritating formaldehyde fumes. Like the well-known little girl in the nursery rhyme, when urea formaldehyde was good, it was very, very good; but when it was bad, it was horrid!

9.7F Molded polystyrene

9.7G Extruded polystyrene

9.7H Polyurethane

THEORY AND REALITY: THE EFFECT OF SLOPPY INSTALLATION

We have just seen that much ingenuity has gone into the industrial creation of dead air. That being the case, the carelessness with which insulation is commonly installed by contractors and homeowners alike never ceases to amaze me. True is the R 4 per inch of still air; but equally true is the reluctance of air to stand still!

Air within or in contact with the thermal envelope is constantly picking up heat from the warm side and losing heat to the cool side. And that same "warm air rising" process which we counted on to carry heat from our wood stove to the most remote areas of our house continues to work wherever air encounters a temperature difference.

The effectiveness of the resulting convective air loops is shown by the R values actually measured across empty 3½"-thick air cavities:

Direction of heat flow	R value of air cavity
up	0.84
sideways	0.91
down	1.22

These R values are dramatically lower than the theoretical R 14 of 3½" of still air. They are also much lower than the R values of 3½" of any of the insulation in Table 9.1.

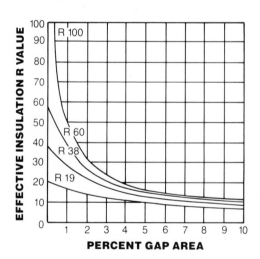

9.8

The incredible heat short-circuiting effect of air gaps in attic insulation is shown by Illustration 9.8. The vertical scale on the left indicates the average or effective attic R value achieved; the horizontal scale along the bottom is the percentage of the attic floor area that consists of air gaps (areas not covered by insulation); and the labeled curves demonstrate the effect of the air gaps on the *nominal* R values of the insulation material installed. The curves show that with a perfect installation (0 percent gap), the effective R values (left scale) are identical to the nominal R values. With just 1 percent of the insulation missing, however, the effective R value drops from R 38 to R 27 and from R 60 to R 38. The short-circuiting effect of a 10 percent gap reduces the effective R values of all insulations in the nominal ranges of R 19 to R 100 down to effective ranges of R 7 to R 11!

This effect has such an impact on most retrofitting efforts that I feel compelled to describe a common and realistic example.

Example. You finally decide to insulate your open attic to R 38. Your house was built in 1900, before the housing industry standardized 16″ and 24″ on-center framing systems, and you find that the attic floor joists are 18″ on-center (sometimes I think builders just counted the number of joists on hand and divided into the length of the building). Down at the lumberyard you find that R 19 fiberglass batts are on sale. Great; you'll install a double layer! Then you discover that they only come in nominal widths of 16″ and 24″. Now the distance between your 2″ thick joists (where you plan to place the insulation) is 18″ − 2″ = 16″, but the actual width of the fiberglass batts is only 15″. Coolly and quickly evaluating the situation so as not to unduly squander the salesman's valuable time (the salesman being an eighteen-year-old kid whose only thought while you're deliberating is how to obtain a six-pack for the evening), you opt for the 15″ batt. After all, 15/16ths is very close to 100 percent! And so you install the batts: 2″ of wood, 15″ of batt, 1″ of air, and so on.

Ignoring the 2 inches of wood, what have you achieved? Your percentage of air gap is 1/16th or 6 percent. Consulting Illustration 9.8, we find that at the 6 percent gap, the nominal R 38 curve has dropped to R 13. That's right, you've just paid for an R 38 attic and gotten R 13! What's the solution? You should have also picked up a bag or two of loose fill insulation to pour into the 1″ air gaps.

The attic example above is probably the most common problem situation encountered. But other problem areas abound: attic access panels, recessed folding stairs, and recessed lighting fixtures; gaps at tops and bottoms of wall stud spaces; gaps around window and door framing; and basement box sills are a few. In the next chapter you'll see through the "eye" of an infrared scanner what the inexorable force of gravity did over a period of forty years to the farmer's blown-in rock-wool wall insulation.

HOW MUCH INSULATION SHOULD ONE INSTALL?

We saw an example of the Law of Diminishing Returns in Chapter 7 when we considered the potential savings of a third glazing layer on our windows. You'll recall that a third glazing increased the R value of a window by 50 percent (from R 2 to R 3), but cut heat loss by only 16 percent (from 1/2 to 1/3). The same law holds true of other forms of insulation.

How does one rationally determine the optimum thickness of insulation to add? By life-cycle costing, obviously!

The true cost of insulating an attic floor, for example, is the total of: (1) the cost of installing the insulation; and (2) the cost of subsequent energy loss through that insulation over its life. Illustration 9.9 shows the life-cycle costs of 3″ increments of short-fiber fiberglass (R 4/inch), contractor-installed over an attic floor with an existing R value of 6. The cost of energy lost in wasted fuel is based on 7,500 heating degree days, $.83/100,000 Btu of delivered heat, and a life of thirty years. Study the illustration closely. The installation cost, which is proportional to the amount of material used, rises steadily. The cost of fuel drops according to the Law of Diminishing Returns. But the total of the two costs drops, reaches a minimum point,

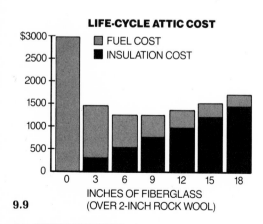

9.9

and then *rises*. This minimum point—at which the insulation thickness results in the minimum life-cycle cost—is our *optimum level of insulation;* in this particular case, a thickness of 6 inches. The total attic R value at that thickness is the initial R 6 plus 6″ × R 4/inch = R 6 + R 24 = R 30.

Through a mathematical nicety the equivalent optimum thickness using other fuels is proportional to the square root of the fuel cost per delivered 100,000 Btu. Using the fuel cost figures from Illustration 3.11, we find:

Heating Fuel	Optimum R
Electric resistance @ $.068/kwh	R 49
Oil @ $1.18/gal	R 38
Natural gas @ $.70/CCF	R 33
Coal @ $125/ton	R 30
Wood @ $100/cord	R 30

Illustration 9.10 is a general guide to optimum ceiling/wall R values throughout the United States, assuming gas or oil heat plus electric air conditioning.

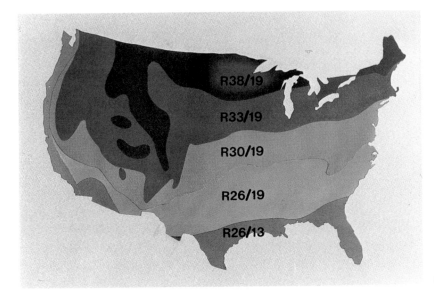

9.10

MOISTURE AND THE NEED FOR VAPOR BARRIERS

The need for vapor barriers, and the role they play, are among the most confusing issues in energy conservation. But don't fear; understanding vapor barriers is no more difficult than watching condensation roll down the outside of a cold mug of beer.

Water exists in three physical states: solid ice, liquid water, and water vapor. Water vapor is the gaseous form of water and is normally found in varying amounts in the air we breathe. Like a sponge, however, air can hold only so much water vapor. Any excess falls out as liquid water. The saturation curve in Illustration 9.11 shows that the amount of water vapor air can hold is a function of the air temperature: the cooler the air, the less water vapor it can hold.

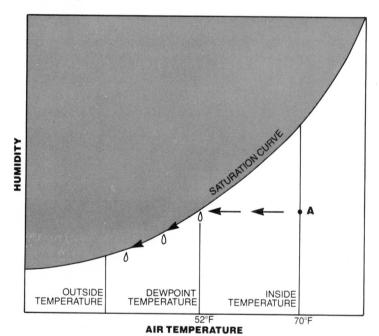

9.11

The *ratio* of the actual amount of water vapor in the air to the amount possible (amount at saturation) is called the relative humidity (RH) of the air. Now suppose, as in the illustration, a parcel of air at 70° and 50 percent RH (Point A) begins to cool. In cooling, it moves horizontally to the left, and as it goes, its RH (relative humidity) increases. As soon as it reaches the saturation curve, its RH is 100 percent, and it can hold no more

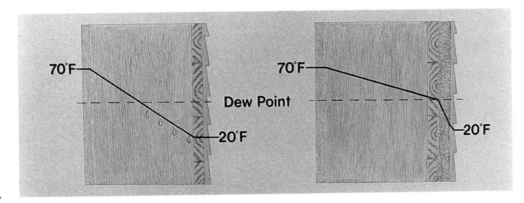

water vapor. Precisely at this point (its *dew point;* 52° in our example), excess water vapor begins to condense out as liquid water droplets.

And that's precisely what you see on your cold mug of beer (presumably the British who drink warm beer have never seen it, but they've seen enough fog, which is the atmospheric equivalent). Air in contact with the cold mug cools to the point where some of its water vapor condenses on the glass. But have you ever seen water on the outer surface of a mug of hot coffee? Not unless your mug has a leak!

The reason is easily seen from Illustration 9.11. Condensation can occur only as air *cools;* it never occurs as air *warms.*

Now, let's look into an insulated wall cavity. Illustration 9.12A shows how the temperature might drop through a wall cavity in winter, from an inside temperature of 70° to an outside temperature of 20°. The rate of temperature drop through materials is proportional to the R value of the material. If the air in the wall cavity originated within the house at 70° and 50 percent RH (point A in Illustration 9.11), the dew point occurs somewhere within the cavity insulation. From that point outward, condensation is possible. Suppose, however, that the wall is further insulated by a layer of foam on the outside. Then the temperature drop occurs across the combined R values of cavity and foam. In Illustration 9.12B, the R value of the foam is more than half of the total R value, and the dew point is reached inside the foam. If the foam is impervious to water vapor (a closed-cell foam), then *no* condensation can possibly occur anywhere!

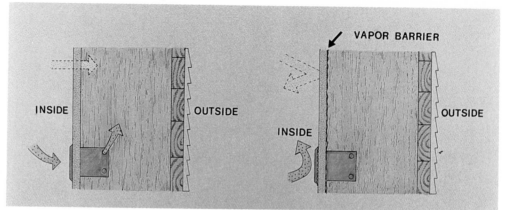

However, the use of exterior foam insulation is a new and relatively unfamiliar construction technique to date, and we in the colder parts of the country have to deal with the possibility of condensation damaging the cavities of our thermal envelopes.

Illustration 9.13 demonstrates the function of a vapor barrier. On the left (without vapor barrier) we see how water vapor gets into the wall cavity in the first place. Water vapor is a gas and, like the helium in a balloon, can very slowly diffuse, or leak, through the apparently solid wall surface. We now recognize that most water vapor actually enters the wall cavity along with room air through holes in the wall surface, such as those in electrical boxes and around trim. A *vapor barrier* is any material impervious to water vapor that is placed on the warmer side of a thermal envelope cavity in order to keep warm inside air from entering the cavity.

Some question has been raised of late as to the importance of vapor barriers in the *average house*. Most households are actually operated at around 65°, 30 percent RH during the winter — not the 70°, 50 percent more typical of greenhouses, as shown in our example above. Under those average conditions, the dew point occurs at a much lower 30°, not 52°. Furthermore, a dynamic state exists in the insulated cavity: condensation (accumulation) when below 30°; and evaporation (dispersion) when above 30°. Overall, condensation in insulated cavities appears to be a problem only in homes run at *relative humidities in excess of 30 percent* and in areas where the *average winter temperature is less than 30°*.

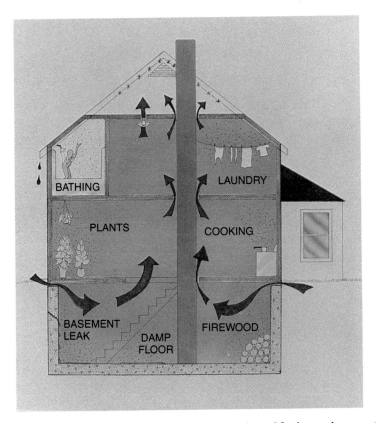

9.14

If the relative humidity in your house in midwinter is greater than 30 percent (easily monitored with a $5 "hygrometer"), you should ask yourself where that water vapor is coming from. If air were merely entering one side of the house and exiting from the other without picking up additional household water vapor, the midwinter indoor RH should read 20 to 30 percent. Any additional moisture must have been picked up inside the house. Illustration 9.14 shows common sources of household moisture. The only guaranteed solution to a condensation problem is putting a lid on moisture-generating activities!

The most commonly applied vapor barrier—polyethylene sheeting—is extremely inexpensive. It may cost an added $200 to $500 to wrap the entire inside surface of the thermal envelope with "poly." Do it! Not only is it condensation insurance; it will quickly pay for itself in terms of reduced infiltration heat loss alone.

VAPOR BARRIER— YES OR NO?

10.   *The Specific Theory of Insulation*

INTRODUCTION

In the last chapter we studied the *general* theory of insulation. We found, much to our amazement, that it is all just so much air. But that air has a special quality not ordinarily possessed by air—it doesn't move.

In this chapter we will study the *specific* theory of insulation; that is, how to insulate properly those large surfaces of the thermal envelope: floors, walls, and ceilings. In so doing, we will apply the principles we've already learned:

- life-cycle cost analysis of options
- elimination of air gaps, however small
- installation of warm-side vapor barriers.

THERMAL ENVELOPE

Illustration 10.1 identifies specifically the thermal envelope of my house. I've decided, because of the extraordinary effort and expense involved in properly retrofitting my barn, that the basement will serve indefinitely as my workshop. Given the estimated $10,000 cost of barn restoration and the number of hours I would probably actually use my workshop, it would be slightly less expensive per hour to lease Boston's Symphony Hall. I also decided to splurge in one area of the house and have a cathedral ceiling in the master bedroom. It costs more to retrofit and more to heat, but I daily become more convinced that I'm only going to live once. So my thermal envelope consists of (starting from the bottom): basement floor, basement wall, bulkhead door, exterior wall, windows, entrance doors, cathedral ceiling, sloping ceiling, attic flat, and attic scuttle. We've already dealt with the doors and windows, and there is nothing worth doing to the basement floor (effective R value of 20–30 already), so our tasks in this chapter are:

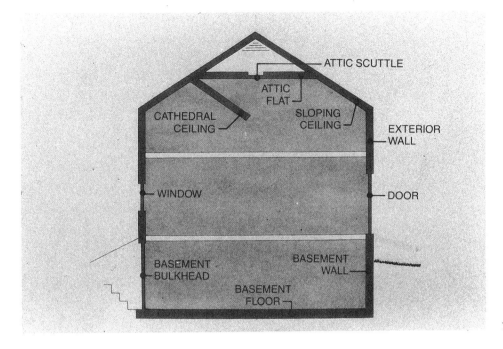

10.1

- basement wall
- exterior wall
- cathedral ceiling
- sloping ceiling
- attic flat.

BASEMENT WALL

The basement is quite dry all year-round, thanks to the well-drained sandy soil and low water table of the old river plain on which we sit. The floor consists of enormous flat stones with concrete in the joints. The walls are also of large stone, from basement floor to about one foot below grade, topped by two feet of brick wall. The stones are placed so that the inside wall surface is fairly smooth, but the outside juts out beyond the brick in a shelf and is extremely irregular.

The nature of the wall dictates my options: (1) do nothing; (2) insulate outside the brick wall with rigid extruded polystyrene; (3) build, insulate, and finish a stud wall inside the stone and brick wall; (4) hang fiberglass batts down the inside surface.

Aside from the costs and fuel savings, which we'll get to presently, the advantages and disadvantages of each are:

1. *Doing nothing* is a piece of cake. Let's hope that proves to be the best solution!

2. *Foam outside*. This is an intriguing retrofit solution that is becoming quite common in new construction. It leaves the quite pleasing (to me) stone and old brick surfaces revealed, and places the massive wall inside the thermal envelope. It also eliminates the thermal short-circuit and air leak associated with the building sill. Two concerns, however, are the uprooting of existing shrubbery and the need to protect the exposed foam surface.

3. *Stud wall*. This solution essentially transforms the basement into a very dark equivalent of the upstairs, but has the disadvantage of removing the masonry walls, with their heat-storing potential, to the outside of the thermal envelope.

4. *Batts only*. Fiberglass is nasty stuff. Confined to a wall cavity or an unused attic, it's great; but please keep it out of my sight — and out of my nose! A second disadvantage is its fragility. For one thing, you can't hang workshop tools from it. Second, assuming human activity in the same vicinity, chances are you'll be replacing it every ten to fifteen years. Third, placing fiberglass between the living space and the masonry wall also removes the very large and useful thermal mass to the outside of the thermal envelope. Placed inside, the wall could help moderate temperature swings in both winter and summer.

Illustration 10.2 shows my life-cycle cost analysis of the four basement wall options. Unfortunately, it appears that doing nothing is a very expensive long-term option! Rigid 1½" exterior foam to three feet below grade raises the R value of the basement wall the least (from R 3 to R 10), but the resulting higher fuel cost is more than offset by a surprisingly low installation cost. The very common solution of framing, insulating, and paneling a wall inside the basement wall has an identical LCC to exterior foam, but eliminates the advantage of placing the masonry inside the thermal envelope. R 19 batts are very inexpensive to buy, but the projected requirement to replace the batts twice in the thirty-year life cycle actually makes their installation the most expensive. I'm pleased to see that LCC points in the direction I already favored — rigid foam installed outside the foundation.

Below, I'll show you how I insulated my basement walls with

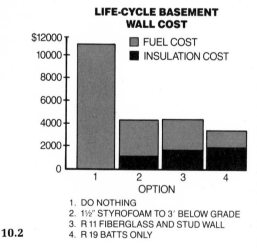

LIFE-CYCLE BASEMENT WALL COST

■ FUEL COST
■ INSULATION COST

OPTION

1. DO NOTHING
2. 1½" STYROFOAM TO 3' BELOW GRADE
3. R 11 FIBERGLASS AND STUD WALL
4. R 19 BATTS ONLY

10.2

extruded polystyrene. Because you're not me, however, I'll also show you how to hang batts on the wall and, for an unheated basement, how to insulate the floor over a basement.

All exterior walls were insulated long ago (eons, apparently) with blown-in rock wool. Removing exterior wall receptacles and switch cover plates revealed the insulation. Such limited detective work can be deceptive, however. I must confess that my feeling of smugness at having an "insulated" house changed to dismay as I viewed the walls through an infrared scanner.

Illustration 10.3 shows what I saw: A, with my naked eye, and then B, through the scanner. The scanner "sees" the temperature of surfaces, warm areas appearing as red and cold areas as black. At the time of the photographs the outdoor temperature was 30° and the inside 70°. The ceiling and lower part of the wall are almost uniformly red (warm), but the top 18 inches of wall is black (cold). The vertical lines appear suspiciously like wall studs. The inescapable conclusion is that the rock wool insulation has settled, leaving 18-inch voids at the top of each stud space.

Considering the effect of air gaps on the overall R value of insulated attics (Illustration 9.8), this was a distressing revelation. Using a formula which you would find distressing, and my 49-function calculator, I rapidly calculated the effective R value of the wall I had previously assumed to be 14. The answer? 6.0! Clearly, something needed to be done.

EXTERIOR WALLS

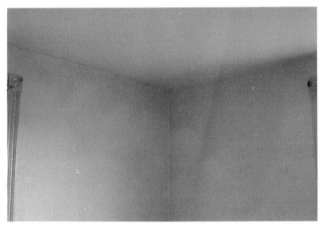

10.3A

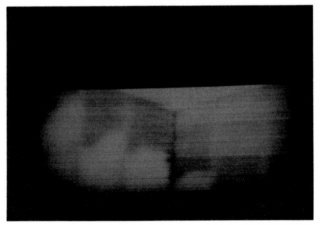

10.3B

While the infrared scanner was in my possession, I entertained myself with a complete tour of the house. Illustration 10.4 shows some of the highlights of my tour:

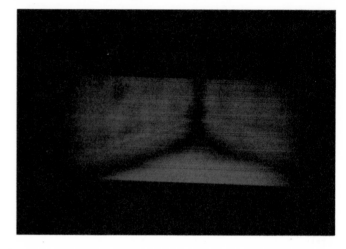

10.4A

A is the base of the same wall, and shows the chilling effects of both air infiltration under the baseboard and the lack of insulation in the corner framing.

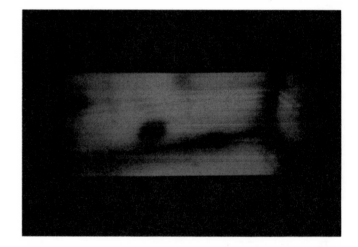

10.4B

B is the base of a wall in another room, showing the same effects as A, plus an infiltration-chilled electrical receptacle.

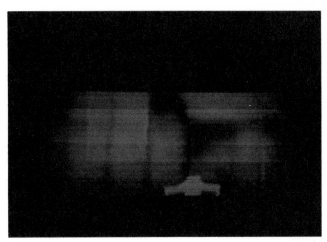

10.4C

C shows a chair at room temperature and the wall cavity with settled insulation in an upstairs room. It also shows that the sloping ceiling is already insulated.

10.4D

D shows just how cold a single-glazed window can be, plus air infiltration around the left rail of the bottom sash.

10.4E

E shows that my old water heater is functioning and losing heat from the hot-water pipe and from the temperature-control panel.

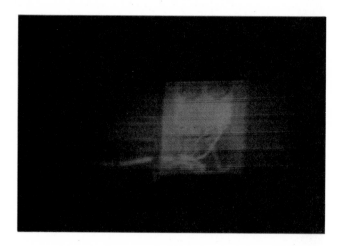

10.4F

F shows which of my four overloaded electric circuits is carrying the most juice—the one that serves the water heater!

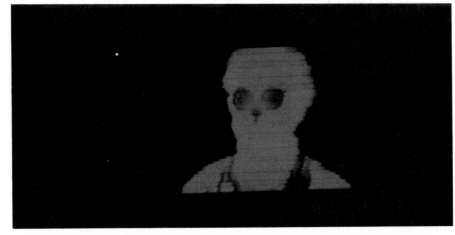

10.4G

G is a self-portrait showing that I have thinning hair, a cold nose, and glasses.

10.4H

H is a winter view of me and my basement wall (I'm the bump). The scanner is telling us that the basement wall is losing heat more rapidly (has a lower R value) than either the wall above or the double-glazed basement window!

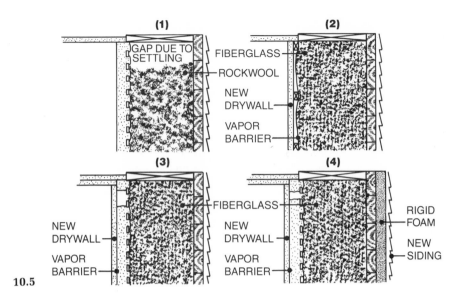

10.5

But back to the walls. Thanks to the extensive surgery we've performed on the window arrangement of the west wall and the razing of the woodshed on the south wall, we have two categories of exterior wall. We have done absolutely nothing to the existing siding and trim on the north and east walls. The exterior changes to the south and west walls, however, are so extensive that entirely replacing the siding would be less expensive than cutting and patching.

I considered the four options shown in Illustration 10.5: (1) do nothing; (2) remove the plaster and lath, strap every 16 inches, and install R 19 batts, poly vapor barrier, and 1/2″ gypsum drywall; (3) blow short-fiber fiberglass into the settled gaps from inside, and install poly vapor barrier and 1/2″ gypsum drywall; (4) same as (3) plus sheath outside of wall with 1″ rigid foam before vinyl siding. Illustration 10.6 shows the LCC analysis.

The high fuel cost of the do-nothing Option 1 proves that the settled wall insulation is well worth repairing. I've removed plaster and lath before, and so was relieved to see the high LCC of Option 2. Options 3 and 4 trade off installation cost with fuel cost and end in a virtual dead heat. Option 4 is appropriate for my south and west walls since I have to re-side the walls there anyway, and Option 3 is best for the north and east walls where the otherwise unnecessary re-siding would add at least $1,000 to the installation cost.

I chose short-fiber fiberglass over cellulose, rock wool, and long-fiber fiberglass because of its immunity to water damage, its ability to fill small gaps, and its high R value per inch. Filling the gaps was especially simple and inexpensive from the inside since I planned to apply poly and drywall right over the existing plaster and wouldn't have to repair any holes. (If you're not applying drywall, the insulation can be almost as easily blown from the outside after removing strips of siding.) We also installed insulation around the window framing by cutting the sash cords, removing the pulleys, blowing through the pulley holes, and then covering with a thin strip of wood.

When the sloping and overhead flat ceilings in the ell were removed, my cathedral ceiling was revealed as ugly, water-stained pine boards supported by rough-sawn 2″ × 6″ rafters spaced 29″ on-center.

Illustration 10.7 shows the four cathedral-ceiling options I considered: (1) do nothing more (an increasingly appealing option); (2) install unfaced 3½″ fiberglass blankets, a poly vapor barrier, and 1/2″ gypsum drywall; (3) install vent channels, 6″ fiberglass batts, 1″ rigid foam, and 1/2″ gypsum drywall; and (4) install on top of the roofing boards 3″ rigid foam, plywood, and new roofing shingles.

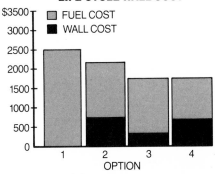

LIFE-CYCLE WALL COST

☐ FUEL COST
■ WALL COST

1. DO NOTHING
2. GUT AND STRAP, PLUS R 19 FIBERGLASS
3. BLOW IN FIBERGLASS
4. BLOW IN FIBERGLASS, PLUS 1″ STYROFOAM

10.6

CATHEDRAL CEILING

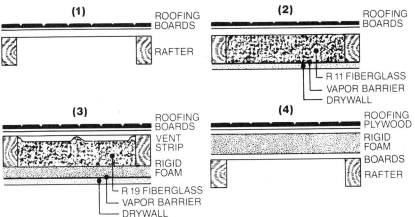

10.7

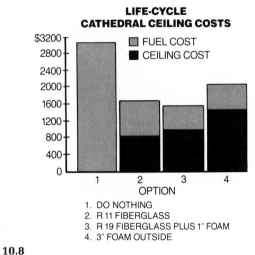

LIFE-CYCLE CATHEDRAL CEILING COSTS

Legend:
- FUEL COST
- CEILING COST

1. DO NOTHING
2. R 11 FIBERGLASS
3. R 19 FIBERGLASS PLUS 1" FOAM
4. 3" FOAM OUTSIDE

10.8

Options 2 and 3 allow air to flow between the insulation and roof boards from a vent strip inlet in the soffit (horizontal board under roof overhang) to a continuous ridge vent outlet. This is a recommended practice when insulating between rafters to prevent moisture condensation under the roof boards, summer overheating of the roof boards, and winter ice-dams. Option 4 prevents all of the above problems by keeping the roof boards inside the thermal envelope.

Illustration 10.8 shows the LCC analysis of the four cathedral-ceiling options. Once again, doing nothing proves to be a luxury I can ill afford; Option 2 is cheap to install but expensive to heat; Option 3 is more expensive to install, but saves enough fuel to have the lowest LCC; Option 4 is high tech, but high cost too, owing to the added cost of new roofing shingles. In a new house, where all the options would require new roofing, Option 4 would be quite competitive. But in my old house I'll go with the LCC Option 3.

SLOPING CEILING AND ATTIC FLAT

As shown in Illustration 10.4C, the sloping ceilings are already insulated with blown rock wool. Blowing insulation between the rafters of a sloping ceiling is not "recommended practice." The potential problems include winter buildup of moisture and summer buildup of heat in the roofing boards. Both phenomena can damage, and require ultimate replacement of, the roof boards. However, the alternatives (identical to those of the cathedral ceiling above) are expensive.

Excessive moisture and excessive heat do not always occur, however. Moisture damage is a function of house humidity and the presence or absence of an effective vapor barrier. In the ceiling, heat damage is a function of roof color, roof orientation, and the degree of shading by nearby trees. In an older house, one can reasonably assume that if damage has not already occurred in an insulated slope, future damage is unlikely. This, fortunately, is my case; and I will be further reducing the risk of condensation by extending the added layer of poly and 1/2" gypsum drywall from the walls to both the sloping and overhead flat ceilings.

The attic flat is typical of an older home. Here we find old wiring, remnants from the past lives of humans and rodents alike, and 2 inches of rock wool. We will be installing an effective vapor barrier on the ceiling below, so the question reduces to how much of what kind of insulation to install.

Illustration 9.8 is a convincing argument for the use of loose-fill insulation in attics with oddball framing. Of the loose fills listed in Table 9.1, short-fiber fiberglass and cellulose stand out for low-cost, high R value per inch, and ability to fill small and irregular spaces. I'll go with the short-fiber fiberglass, even at slightly higher cost, because of its completely inert nature and because I'm already using it in the side walls.

Illustration 10.9 shows the LCC of my attic options—in this case, in increments of insulation thickness. This same analysis was used to determine the optimum thickness of insulation in Chapter 9. Based on a heating cost per delivered 100,000 Btu of $0.83, a thirty-year life, and 7,500 heating degrees days, my minimum LCC occurs at a thickness of 6 inches. Adding the 6 inches at R 4 per inch to the existing R 6 of the old rock wool gives me an optimum R 30.

Note, however, that the LCC at 9 inches (total of R 42) is just slightly higher. Remembering that utility companies were awarding gold stars (or some such thing) to customers who installed R 19 batts in their attics only ten years ago, I think I'll go that extra 3 inches!

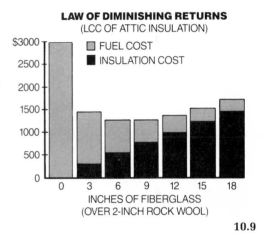

LAW OF DIMINISHING RETURNS
(LCC OF ATTIC INSULATION)

■ FUEL COST
■ INSULATION COST

INCHES OF FIBERGLASS
(OVER 2-INCH ROCK WOOL)

10.9

Insulating wall cavities and ceilings is best left to contractors. Besides, it's pretty common fare, and I want this book to be exciting.

I think the most exciting discovery in this chapter is the importance of insulating basements. For that reason, I'm going to show you how to draw the defense line against basement heat loss in three optional places: (1) between the floor joists; (2) inside the basement wall; and (3) outside the basement wall.

HOW TO DO IT

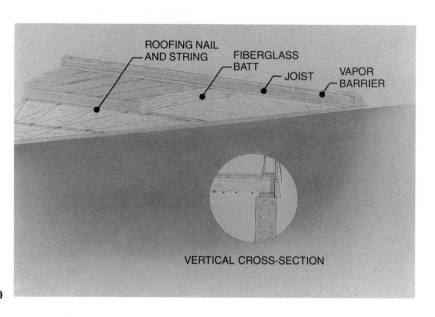

ROOFING NAIL
AND STRING

FIBERGLASS
BATT

JOIST

VAPOR
BARRIER

VERTICAL CROSS-SECTION

10.10

Insulating Between the Floor Joists
(Illustration 10.10)

Provided you are *sure* you want an unheated basement or crawl space and that your pipes won't freeze, you can stop the downward heat loss from your thermal envelope at the floor over the basement.

STEP 1. Measure the spacing between the floor joists. Cut strips of clear 4- or 6-mil polyethylene 4″ wider than the joist space. Staple the poly strips up against the subfloor with 2″ overlapped against the joists. (Don't enclose the entire joist, as the poly exposed at the joist bottom would find itself on the cold side and collect moisture from the house.)

STEP 2. Install roofing nails every 6″ to 8″ along the bottoms of the joists. Leave the heads projecting by 1/4″.

STEP 3. Cut 9″ (R 30) fiberglass batts 1/2″ to 1″ wider than the joist space. (If joists are irregularly spaced, measure and cut one batt at a time). Batts are easily cut with a sharp French cooking knife, using a long board both to compress the insulation and to serve as a straightedge. If the joist space is wider than 23″, run the batts in the other direction, cutting sections of batt 1″ longer than the width of the joist space.

STEP 4. Fit the batts carefully but snugly up against the subfloor to eliminate air spaces and zigzag baling wire or nylon mason's twine between the roofing nails. Carefully cut and fit insulation around interfering pipes, wires, and bridging. Remember—no air gaps!

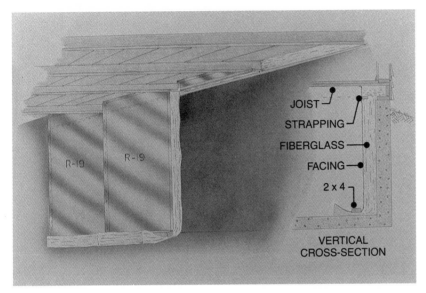

JOIST

STRAPPING

FIBERGLASS

FACING

2 x 4

R-19   R-19

VERTICAL
CROSS-SECTION

Provided you never use your basement, and provided you don't need the thermal mass of the masonry wall, the simplest way to insulate a basement wall is by covering it with a fiberglass blanket.

STEP 1. First, you must solve the problem of the sill. The illustration shows a box sill. The solution is to cut and fit batts of unfaced fiberglass into the cavity. Do not use a vapor barrier yet.

STEP 2. Nail 1″ × 3″ strapping under and at right angles to the floor joists about 6″ in from and parallel to the masonry wall. On the walls running parallel to the joists, build out the wood sill to 2″–4″ beyond the masonry.

STEP 3. Staple the foil facing of a section of fiberglass blanket to the subfloor above, the strapping below, and the joists on the sides.

STEP 4. Staple foil-faced fiberglass to the strapping above and let it hang down to and spill onto the floor by 12″.

10.11

Insulating Inside the Basement Wall
(Illustration 10.11)

STEP 5. Overlap the adjacent flanges of the facing and staple together, using an office-type stapler.

STEP 6. Place lengths of strapping or 2 × 4s over the fiberglass on the floor. This prevents cold air behind the fiberglass from escaping at the bottom.

If you have followed all of the above steps correctly, you have created a uniform blanket of insulation from subfloor to basement floor, with a complete vapor barrier on the warm side.

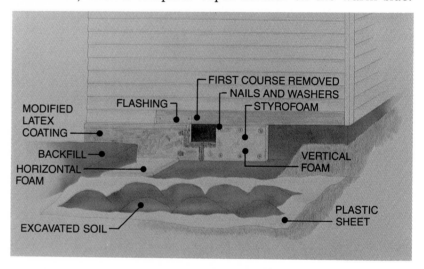

10.12

Insulating Outside the Basement Wall
(Illustration 10.12)

The very best way to stop downward heat flow is to insulate outside the basement wall. Insulating outside the wall places the massive basement wall inside the thermal envelope, where it can help to moderate building temperature swings, both winter and summer.

Because of a combination of strength and impermeability to moisture, the only type of insulation suitable for this application is extruded polystyrene.

STEP 1. Remove several bottom courses of siding from all around the building. Consult a blown-in insulation contractor about the best method. They confront this task daily.

STEP 2. First, dig up and wrap the root balls of valued shrubs. Then, excavate a strip around the entire building perimeter 1′ deep and 2′ to 4′ wide, placing the excavated soil on a sheet of polyethylene. Call an excavation contractor for an estimate on the digging, which can typically be done with a backhoe in several hours.

STEP 3. Brush off the exposed masonry. If you live in termite country, now is the time to have a termite poison sprayed onto the masonry wall. The foam will protect the poison, which will, in turn, forever block termites from crawling up between foam and foundation. Then fasten sheets of extruded polystyrene to the wall, using appropriate masonry fasteners and fender washers (big washers with small holes). On a concrete wall use hardened masonry nails fired from a "nail gun." I nailed ordinary galvanized 16-penny nails into the mortar joints of my brick wall. Nail every 2′ on-center.

STEP 4. This is the most crucial step for long-term success. Completely scour the tough, smooth surface of the foam with a wire brush. This provides a fresh, clean, rough surface for the protective coating to sink its "teeth" into. Otherwise you may have later bubbling and peeling of the protective coating.

STEP 5. Apply self-adhesive fiberglass drywall joint tape (available at lumberyards) over all points of stress: exposed edges, corners, joints, and recessed nails and washers.

STEP 6. Install flashing, which will cap the foam and prevent water from entering between foam and masonry wall. You may be able to use the standard aluminum flashing sold for use above doors and windows. I contracted a local sheet-metal shop to bend a galvanized flashing to my specification, and I recommend this technique. Show them a sketch of what you're doing with exact dimensions. Nail to building sheathing with aluminum (for aluminum flashing) or galvanized (for galvanized flashing) roofing nails.

STEP 7. Apply one of the cement-latex finishes recommended by the foam manufacturer for such application. These coatings consist of a mixture of cement, sand, latex, color, and glass fibers; when dry they form a very tough, long-lasting protective skin over the foam. Rigid panels applied with mastic to the foam are also available. In either case, apply the protective finish from the flashing to several inches below the planned ground level.

STEP 8. At this point you have prevented 60–80 percent of your basement heat loss. Stop here if you don't want to disrupt valued plantings. If heat savings are all-important, however, you'll want to continue insulating the ground horizontally away from the foundation. A rule of thumb is to insulate below grade and out from the foundation a combined total distance equal to the local frost depth: for example, 1′ below grade plus 2′ out for a frost depth of 3′.

Smooth and compact the soil, sloping 1″ per foot away from the foundation (to drain rainwater away from the basement); place horizontal sheets of foam and cover with at least 12″ of soil (so that plants can grow).

STEP 9. Grade the soil away from the foundation, plant grass seed and mulch with old hay. Finally, replace the bottom rows of siding.

11. *Hidden Heat Leaks*

INTRODUCTION

Viewed from a distance, or in an architect's plan, a house looks so perfect! So far, with the exception of windows and doors, we have largely ignored the fact that houses are actually put together by dozens of tradespeople from thousands of imperfect pieces, and then inhabited by real people. We are aware of the heat-loss term "infiltration," and of the statistic that most houses suffer a complete loss of conditioned air every one to two hours, whether heated or cooled. But what we don't realize is that windows and doors account for only 10 to 20 percent of the total infiltration; that 80 to 90 percent of air infiltration occurs through other unspecified air leaks.

We call these *hidden heat leaks.* Nobody hid them by design; they are there to see, plain as day. We don't see them because we don't know where to look. But finding hidden heat leaks is no more difficult than finding hidden jelly beans—it's a snap, provided you have a list of their hiding places!

A hidden-heat-leak hunt can be immensely rewarding. If you perform a thorough retrofit, as we just have, a high level of awareness and careful attention to detail will prevent them from ever occurring. But if your task is plugging the leaks in an otherwise attractive existing home, then this chapter may prove the most useful of all.

All you need is a weekend or two of grubbing about in your home's most unpleasant spaces, armed with an easy-to-assemble tool kit of scissors, staple gun, and putty knife. Applying small pieces of fiberglass batting, polyethylene sheeting, and duct tape in places you probably never thought of could save you as much as 25 percent of your present heating and cooling bills.

If that idea appeals to you, grab your tools, lay in your supplies, and take a tour of your house with our list of heat-leak hiding places as your guide.

TOOLS FOR FINDING LEAKS

Professional heat-leak hunters—often called "house doctors"—use very sophisticated and expensive tools to locate heat leaks accurately and rapidly.

The *blower door*, a calibrated, high-speed fan set into an adjustable door frame, is used to blow air under pressure into the house. Natural air leaks are thus magnified by a factor of twenty or more.

The *smoke pencil* emits a very white stream of neutral density "smoke." Unlike the hot, buoyant smoke from a cigarette, this smoke marks and indicates natural air motion. Air blown by the blower door escapes into the cracks and holes of the thermal envelope; the leaks are thus readily "seen" by the smoke pencil.

The *infrared scanner* "sees" objects and surfaces in terms of their temperatures. Illustrations 10.3 and 10.4 are typical of what the viewer sees through a scanner. With a sensitivity of 0.1°, the scanner can readily detect cold surfaces produced by either infiltration or missing insulation.

You may wish to utilize the services of a house doctor, either to detect and mark your heat leaks for you, or to fix them as well. However, just as it doesn't require a CAT scan to diagnose a hangover, you don't need to enlist a professional heat-leak hunter to diagnose your hidden heat leaks. A little common sense will go a long way. Here's how to use your common sense:

STEP 1. Open this book to the list of heat-leak hiding spots below.

STEP 2. Close and lock all of your doors and windows and fireplace dampers.

STEP 3. Turn on all bathroom and kitchen ventilating fans. Set your clothes dryer to "air only" and turn it on. And, if you have an oil-fired furnace or boiler, tape shut the barometric damper and turn the system on by raising the house thermostat. All of the above devices will blow air out of the house and create a magnified infiltration *into* the house which is almost as effective as that created by the blower door.

STEP 4. Grab a wet sponge and, starting in the basement, hold your moistened palm up to any suspected air leak. If air is flowing in, you'll feel it!

Below are a list of thirty common heat leaks and a picture. These are just the most common leaks, mind you; be on the lookout for others. Once you get the hang of the hunt, I'm sure you'll find several unique violations of your personal thermal envelope.

If you use the pressurization technique above, you'll want to conduct the hunt quickly, and return to do the leak plugging later. Record the leaks on predrawn sketches of each floor plan, and mark the leaks themselves with colored tape or chalk.

THE HEAT-LEAK HIT LIST — AND WHAT TO DO WHEN YOU FIND ONE

11.1

17

Basement Areas

1. Bulkhead door. Seal between the door frame and the masonry wall with nonhardening caulk or foam caulk. Large gaps can be stuffed with fiberglass. Don't forget to insulate and weatherstrip the door itself as shown in Chapter 6.

2. Basement windows. Seal between the wood frame and masonry wall, and the wood frame and sill overhead, with caulk. Consider blocking off the window with panels of rigid foam in winter or installing an inside-type storm window as described in Chapter 7.

3. Sill plate. Seal cracks between the wood sill and the top of the masonry foundation with either foam caulk or strips of fiberglass applied with a putty knife. Seal from *both* inside and outside if possible (this is a *big* one).

4. Outside faucet. Stuff large holes first with fiberglass; then caulk with silicone. Do both inside and out.

5. Electric service cable. Do the same as in Item 4 to the large-diameter cable running from your electric meter into the house. Again, seal outside *and* inside if accessible.

6. Telephone cable. Trace where the typically small round white wire passes into the house. A dab of silicone should do it.

7. Barometric damper. This is another *big* one! Whenever you're not using your heating system, the barometric damper (see Chapter 4) is not needed. So during the off season, or if you heat only with wood, tape that devil shut!

8. Chimney clean-out. At the base of a masonry chimney you should find a tiny black door that facilitates removal of soot, dead birds, etc. That's a door to the outside! Make sure it fits well and is closed.

Living Areas

9. Doors. Follow the directions in Chapter 6 for major fixes. Also, fill unused keyholes with foam caulk; and — I'm not kidding — fill a sock with a wad of fiberglass and stuff it into the mail slot.

10. Windows. First, read and follow the directions in Chapter 7 for major fixes to windows. Also, caulk with high-quality nonhardening sealant around the outside perimeter where trim meets siding. Caulk around inside perimeter where trim meets wall surface with drywall joint compound or putty. Consider cutting sash cords, removing pulleys, and covering pulley holes with wood or duct tape. Of course, always keep glazing and putty in good repair.

11. Baseboards. Right behind the baseboard is the soleplate of the wall, and boy, does that leak air! Removing and replacing the hundreds of feet of baseboard is time-consuming and difficult. If you really want to try it, though, drive the finish nails all the way through the baseboard, using a "punch" of the same diameter; this is the only way to avoid marring or splitting the wood. Otherwise, "caulk" the cracks between baseboard and floor and baseboard and wall by stuffing lengths of yarn into the spaces with a putty knife.

12. Wall receptacles. Behind your receptacle cover plates are little boxes resembling Swiss cheese. You can at least slow the flow through these holes by installing foam gaskets (available at hardware stores) behind the cover plates.

13. Wall switches. Foam gaskets are also available for installation behind switch plates.

14. Television antenna. You may have cable TV now, but chances are that a flat lead-in wire still penetrates your outside wall somewhere. Even if the wire doesn't, the hole remains. Trace the cable to where it enters the house and caulk both inside and outside surfaces.

15. Cable television. If you have cable TV, you have a round black cable about 1/4″ in diameter penetrating your envelope somewhere. When you find it, don't be deceived by the disk-shaped bushing; it's a hidden heat leak! Pull the bushings (both inside and out) away from the wall and caulk the holes around the cable; then replace the bushings.

16. Medicine cabinet. Is your gargle cold in the winter? If so, your medicine cabinet is probably exchanging air with the stud space around it. Remove the cabinet, insulate behind it, and wrap a plastic vapor barrier around its back and sides before reinstalling.

17. Knee-wall drawers. A knee wall is the short wall upstairs in a Cape or a story-and-a-half house. Sometimes an inner finished wall is constructed several feet in front of the outside unfinished wall. The space between the two walls becomes essentially stud space. Consequently, any drawers built into the wall become doors to the outside. The solution is to either: (1) insulate and vapor-barrier the *outside* wall, or (2) eliminate the built-ins; then insulate and vapor-barrier the *inside* wall.

18. Air conditioner. Whether installed through the wall or in a window, an air conditioner should either be removed for the winter, or wrapped and sealed with poly and duct tape.

19. Range hood. Some ventilating fans have "positive closure" outside lids, or dampers, that are closed manually from inside. Unfortunately, the standard range hood has only a gravity or weak spring-actuated lid. Substituting a stronger spring is no solution, because the fan would then not be able to force the damper open. Unless you replace the standard model with a "ductless" range hood, the best you can do is to keep the damper mechanism clean.

20. Bathroom fan. A powered bath fan venting to the outside has the same problem as the range hood. However, a model with positive closure could be substituted. Also available are air-to-air heat exchangers, which transfer heat from outgoing air to incoming air through the thin membranes separating the air flows. Approximately 75 percent of the heat loss is thus recovered. A 100 percent efficient solution — and a cheaper one, to boot — is to ventilate the bathroom into the basement, provided the basement is large enough and dry enough to absorb the moisture.

21. Clothes-dryer vent. This vent wins the prize for heat-wasting potential. First, it obviously blows all that expensive electric or gas heat outdoors before it can warm us. Second, I can guarantee that, even when the dryer is not operating, the four-inch vent is stuck in the open position. Recently, I removed all the lint from my damper hinges and returned one month later to find the damper jammed open again!

I'm trying two solutions in my retrofitted house. First, I'm retrofitting the backyard with a solar clothes dryer — a 100′ length of rope and 2 pulleys hooked to the nearest tree. Second, for rainy-day use of the electric dryer, I'm venting the dryer outlet to the furnace return duct. While operating the dryer, I will also switch the furnace blower from "auto" to "on" and circulate the damp dryer air throughout the total 22,000-cubic-foot volume of the house, which will easily absorb the moisture (not recommended for gas).

22. Fireplace damper. Have you peered up into the throat of your fireplace lately? The fireplace damper is yet another door to the outside. Two solutions to a damper that doesn't seal well are: (1) stuff the cracks with unfaced fiberglass and hang a sign on the mantel reading "Don't Use," and (2) install glass fireplace doors and caulk the frame to the masonry with fiberglass strips.

Attic Areas

23. Door to attic. We pointed out in Chapter 6 that, if your attic is unheated and ventilated, your attic door opens to the outside. Treat it like any other outside door. If you use it rarely, consider stapling foil-faced fiberglass or nailing a sheet of rigid foam to the attic side.

24. Attic scuttle. Again, this is just a little door to the outside, but don't let its size fool you.

25. Ceiling fan. Whole-house or ceiling fans are designed to move air, not stop it! In winter, build an insulated cover panel to install under the fan, or an insulated box to install over the fan.

26. Recessed light fixtures. These fixtures are notorious heat-wasters. The fire code requires a 3″ clearance on all sides of recessed lighting fixtures. If the ventilating air flow through the fixture and into the attic were blocked, heat from the electric bulb could accumulate to the point of melting the insulating jacket on the wiring or igniting nearby wood. This type of light fixture adds insult to injury by leaking not only warm house air to the attic, but 95 percent of the electric heat of the bulb, as well. The solution? Install a dropped ceiling fixture and stuff the remaining recessed opening with fiberglass.

27. Space around chimney. The fire code also specifies a 2″ clearance between a masonry chimney and combustible materials, such as wood framing. The result is a chimney heat collector, similar to a solar collector, which generates warm air from both chimney and its enclosing walls. This warm air rises up into the attic from around the chimney in an absolute torrent of Btu's. The simple solution is to wedge unfaced fiberglass around the chimney at attic-floor level.

28. Plumbing stack vent. One or more large pipes pass through your ceiling and roof to vent your plumbing system. First spot them on the roof from outside. Then find where they pass through the upper surface of your thermal envelope — whether attic floor or sloping ceiling. Stuff fiberglass between the pipe and opening.

29. Interior walls. Instead of constructing interior partitions on the floor and then raising them into place, carpenters sometimes used to build interior walls, stud by stud, in place. The result was an interior wall without a top plate, or cap on the top. Warm air generated by contact with the warm wall surfaces flows unimpeded directly into the attic. The solution is to cap the open wall at attic-floor level with poly followed by attic insulation, or to blow the interior wall full at the same time as the attic floor.

Duplex houses sometimes have separating "party" walls of hollow concrete block that extend from ground level to roof. Heat readily convects through the empty, interconnected blocks from the warm spaces below to the attic and roof. The solution is to drill holes in the masonry blocks at ceiling level and blow them full of foam insulation.

30. Ducts in unconditioned spaces. Both warm-air heating systems and cooling systems operate as "open loops"; that is, they circulate conditioned air from the system through supply ducts to the house, and back through return ducts to the system. These ducts do not always lie within the thermal envelope. Such ducts are often found in unheated basements, crawl spaces, and attics. A leak in a duct located outside the thermal envelope is still a leak in the thermal envelope. The solution requires three steps: (1) caulk all duct seams; (2) apply duct tape over the caulked seams; (3) insulate the ducts with 2″ (R 6) fiberglass duct-wrap.

Did you get them all? If so, you've just reduced your infiltration by half and doubled your comfort. Cut yourself a little silver star out of duct tape and staple it to your pocket!

12. Hot Water

In the last eleven chapters we have analyzed, insulated, caulked, weatherstripped, and tweaked our thermal envelope and our heating and cooling systems to provide a comfortable space at the lowest possible life-cycle cost. And we have done well. We have lowered our combined heating and cooling bill by an estimated 83 percent, from an annual $2,167 down to $372. But there is one big bill left—our domestic hot-water bill. Unless we take similar action on the hot-water front, our estimated present bill of $454 will outweigh the cost of space conditioning.

Have faith. As you may suspect, our old electric water-heating system is ripe for retrofit. Let's see how well we can do!

INTRODUCTION

What sorts of things are we doing when we mindlessly turn that hot-water spigot? Because most of us don't think about hot-water costs day-to-day, we sometimes put hot water to rather bizarre uses. I know someone who heats his house with wood, and preheats his frigid bathroom by running a hot (and unoccupied) shower for fifteen minutes every morning. Another of my neighbors likes to melt, rather than shovel, the snow from his driveway with hot water from a hose. And, soon after moving into my previous house, I noticed that the toilet was always pleasantly warm; the former owner had solved the problem of toilet tank condensation by running hot water to the toilet!

Most of you will agree that those uses are terribly wasteful. But what about the uses we have come to regard as essential for the maintenance of civilized life? We will examine the degree to which these uses are indeed minimal and essential below, but first, let's all agree that we use hot water for:

HOT-WATER USES

• **Bathing** (Illustration 12.1). Mixed with cold water to achieve a temperature of 105°, the average four-inch bath consumes about 15 gallons of hot water. Can you imagine what those Hollywood-style bubblebaths consume?

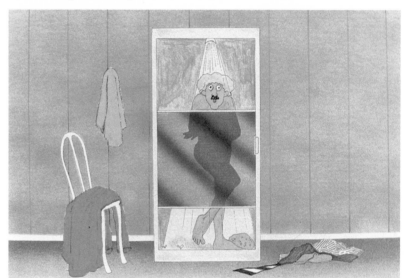

• **Showering** (Illustration 12.2). We've all heard that showers save hot water. I'm not so sure. The average showerhead puts out a life-threatening deluge of 5 to 7 gallons per minute. At that rate, it would take only three to four minutes for a shower to fill an average bathtub. The last time I saw anyone take a three-minute shower was when my water heater died.

12.3

- **Clothes washing** (Illustration 12.3). A single hot wash–cold rinse clothes-washer load consumes 25 gallons of hot water. Today cold water cleans as well as hot and leaves fewer wrinkles in your permanent press clothes. If you *really* want to kill germs, dry your laundry in the ultraviolet rays of the sun.

12.4

- **Dishwashing** (Illustration 12.4). Washing dishes by hand may save hot water—at least, I always thought so, until I discovered that the ten-minute stream of rinse water used by my human dishwashers was *hot water!* I now think it was a plot conceived by those dishwashers to modernize my ways.

12.5

• **Cooking** (Illustration 12.5). We use hot water to rinse veggies, get the spaghetti water to boil faster, and to preheat coffee cups. All these little habits account for a surprising 3 gallons per day on the average.

12.6

• **Washing-shaving** (Illustration 12.6). Removing the bristles from my face once a day requires a gallon of hot water. And that doesn't count the 3 gallons I draw before the water gets hot. I think my hot-water pipe does three laps around the house before it arrives at my upstairs bathroom.

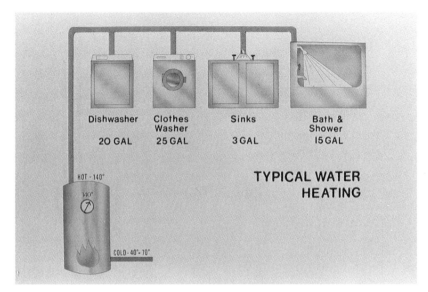

Dishwasher
20 GAL

Clothes Washer
25 GAL

Sinks
3 GAL

Bath & Shower
15 GAL

TYPICAL WATER HEATING

HOT - 140°

140°

COLD - 40° - 70°

12.7

HOW DO HOT-WATER SYSTEMS WORK?

Where does hot water come from? Illustration 12.7 shows a typical water heating and distribution system.

For most of us, water arrives through a copper pipe from somewhere under the street in front of our homes. The temperature of the incoming water varies with the season, since it is a function of the temperature of the source (lake, river, or well) and the depth of the water supply pipe. Over the course of an entire year, the average incoming water temperature is very close to the average annual temperature of the atmosphere. My water is coldest in the early spring, after the intense cold of the winter air has succeeded in freezing the first 4 feet of earth above the water main; the warmest temperature is also delayed by several months after the maximum atmospheric temperatures of July.

The average annual temperature here in Maine is about 45° — cold enough to chill anyone's fillings — so, we direct one branch of the cold-water pipe to a water heater.

TYPES

There are as many ways to heat water as there are to heat a house. And the workings of water heaters are quite similar to the workings of water-based or hydronic heating systems.

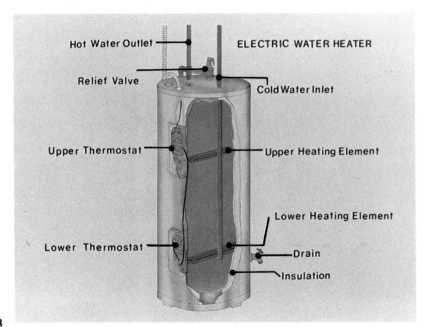

Hot Water Outlet

Relief Valve

ELECTRIC WATER HEATER

Cold Water Inlet

Upper Thermostat

Upper Heating Element

Lower Heating Element

Lower Thermostat

Drain

Insulation

12.8

• **Electric water heater.** Illustration 12.8 shows what goes on inside an electric water heater. Cold water may enter at the bottom of the tank or at the top, as shown, but it is always released at the bottom in order not to disturb the already heated water floating at the top.

Most tanks have two separately controlled heating elements. The lower element comes on after just a few gallons have been withdrawn and the colder temperature of the incoming water is sensed. If enough water is withdrawn for the cold water to reach the upper thermostat, the lower element switches off and the upper element switches on, so that you can draw hot water after heating only the upper portion of the tank. Hot water is drawn from the very top of the tank where the water is always hottest. Because they can produce only about 25 gallons per hour, electric tanks are usually larger than gas and oil tanks.

At the bottom of the tank is a drain valve with hose threads. In case you're wondering what the threads are for, water-heater manufacturers assume incorrectly that homeowners will obediently drain off the sediment at the bottom of the tank once per month through a hose in accordance with those little instructions on the warranty card. At the top of the tank is another valve, which looks like a steam whistle. Its function is to fill your basement with steam instead of tank parts in case one of the thermostats dies in the "on" position.

Between the outer thin metal jacket and the inner tank is a layer of insulation designed to keep most of the heat in the hot water.

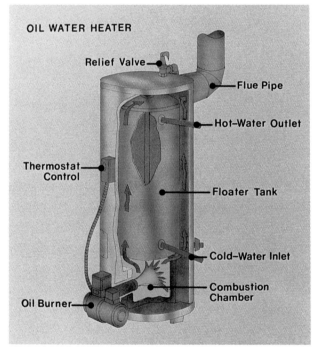

OIL WATER HEATER

Relief Valve
Flue Pipe
Hot–Water Outlet
Thermostat Control
Floater Tank
Cold–Water Inlet
Combustion Chamber
Oil Burner

12.9

• **Oil water heater.** Illustration 12.9 is of an oil-fired water heater. It looks like a cheaper version of an oil boiler (see Chapter 4). It is less expensive because the heat exchanger consists of nothing more than the surface of the hot-water tank, separating hot flue gases from the cooler water. There is only one thermostat to control the single oil burner, but, because of the high rate of burner heat output (minimum of 50,000 Btu/hr.), the average oil water heater is capable of delivering a continuous 100 gallons of hot water per hour. As with the hydronic boiler, the standby loss (loss of heat to air flowing through the burner, past the tank, and out the flue pipe) is much larger than in the case of the flueless electric tank.

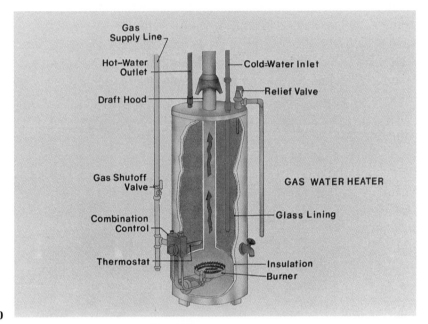

Gas
Supply Line

Hot–Water
Outlet

Cold–Water Inlet

Draft Hood

Relief Valve

Gas Shutoff
Valve

GAS WATER HEATER

Combination
Control

Glass Lining

Thermostat

Insulation
Burner

12.10

• **Gas water heater** (Illustration 12.10). Gas water heaters are also similar to their hydronic space-heating counterparts. Even though they resemble boilers, their extreme simplicity and small size (average 40-gallon tank) make them no more expensive than electric water heaters. Because until recently gas had the lowest fuel cost, the gas water heater is found in more homes than any other. Like the oil heater, gas heaters tend to have large flue standby losses, and automatic vent dampers are sometimes installed between the draft hood and flue pipe.

• **Oil and gas tankless heaters** were described in Chapter 4. These are simple coils of heat-exchanger pipe immersed in the space-heating boiler water jacket that heats the domestic hot water. Although they are inexpensive and efficient during the winter heating season, they turn into energy-gobblers during the summer because of the large standby loss of the overly large boiler. Some perceptive tankless owners switch to electric or solar water heaters during the summer.

• **Electric heat pump.** The heat pump works just like a refrigerator. It draws heat energy out of a relatively cool medium and then releases it into a warmer medium. Usually, the cool medium is basement air, and the warmer medium is the water in an electric water heater tank. In fact, 2 to 3 Btu's of basement air heat can be "pumped" into the water for each Btu of electricity consumed by the pump, leading to a water-heating efficiency of 200 to 300 percent. Whether you can credit the heat pump with a full 300 percent efficiency depends, however, on the value of the heat withdrawn from the basement air. If you heat your basement electrically, you are gaining precisely nothing; if your basement is unheated — and provided the loss of heat to the heat pump won't cause your pipes to freeze — then a heat pump might be a good solution. Savings are likely to be highest in southern states where the heat pump can air-condition a house at the same time it heats the hot water.

• **Spot or tankless water heaters.** Not to be confused with boiler tankless water heaters, these heaters without storage tanks have been used in Europe for decades to produce hot water on demand without incurring tank standby losses. They are often located close to the major point of use, thereby also eliminating the loss of heat from hot water stranded in supply pipes.

While actually heating water, they are no more efficient at converting CCF's of gas and kwh's of electricity to hot-water Btu's than their tank-type counterparts. Economies are realized, therefore, primarily in low-consumption situations.

• **Solar water heaters.** A typical solar domestic hot-water heater for the northern half of the United States consists of a double-glazed collector (black-painted water piping insulated on sides and back and covered with 1 or 2 layers of glass), a storage tank (80–120-gallon tank for a full day's use with an electric backup element for cloudy days), and a system for exchanging heat between the collector and storage tank (thermostatically controlled to prevent either freezing or heat flowing in the wrong direction). Properly sized for the level of hot-water consumption, such a system can be expected to provide 20 to 30 percent of the hot water demand in winter and 100 percent in summer, for an overall annual fraction of 50 to 60 percent. The typical installed cost for a system consisting of a 50–60-square-foot collector and an 80–120-gallon storage tank is $4,000, or $2,400 after the 40 percent federal income tax credit. Compared to the water heaters above, solar system equipment is expensive, but its effective fuel price is cheap. Whether it pays off depends on the cost of the competing fuel and, more importantly, on the amount of hot water consumed.

HOW MUCH ENERGY IS USED IN HEATING HOT WATER?

Like space-heating systems, most domestic hot-water heaters suffer standby losses in addition to the energy actually used to heat water. Referring to Illustration 12.7, you can see several areas of potential standby loss:

- For fuel-fired systems, losses up the flue pipe while the unit is not actually firing.
- Tank jacket losses to the surrounding air. Unlike the space-heating system, even a water tank located in a heated space suffers costly loss in the summer.
- Pipe losses of two sorts: radiation from the first few feet of copper pipe projecting from the tank; and loss of heat from water stranded in piping after water is drawn.

These standby losses all together amount to several million Btu per year, or 15 to 20 percent of the typical hot-water bill. Since standby losses are nearly independent of the amount of hot water consumed, we'll find that they become increasingly important as consumption is decreased.

To calculate the energy used in the primary task of raising the temperature of the water is a simple matter. Recalling the definition of the Btu—the amount of heat required to raise the temperature of a pound (a pint) of water by 1°—all we need to do is multiply the number of pints per year by the average temperature boost in degrees. Assuming the average American consumption of about 65 gallons per day and temperature rise from 60° to 140°:

$$
\begin{aligned}
\text{Btu} &= (\text{pints per year}) \times (\text{temperature rise}) \\
&= (65 \text{ gal.} \times 8 \text{ pints} \times 365 \text{ days}) \times (140° - 60°) \\
&= 15{,}000{,}000 \text{ Btu}
\end{aligned}
$$

LOWERING THE HOT-WATER BILL

There are three categories of hot-water retrofit. As in space-heating, each retrofit category costs progressively more. The three categories detailed below are:

- Conservation—in other words, "retrofitting" our slothful habits.
- System retrofit—adjusting and insulating against standby losses.
- Major surgery—installing a new, more efficient system.

CONSERVATION

Believe it or not, people didn't always have hot water at the tap! When I bought my first old farmhouse in Maine, my wife and I searched high and low for the water heater. Thinking that the previous owner had absconded with it, it never occurred to us that life was tolerable without one. Checking around the neighborhood, I found that many of our neighbors heated their Saturday-night bathwater in a large kettle on the wood stove.

I am not advocating that we live without hot water; I am merely pointing out that examining the ways we presently use hot water may be profitable. Since it costs us nothing to use less hot water, it certainly promises to be a cost-effective activity.

I can break our hot-water usage into five categories (general, showering, bathing, clothes-washing, and automatic dishwashing). Illustration 12.11 compares my family's present daily consumption to a hypothetical consumption level if we were to retrofit our life-style. General usage would drop by 50 percent through the use of faucet aerators and more conscientious tap operation; baths would be eliminated in favor of showers, and shower consumption would be cut in half by installing water-saving showerheads; all clothes could be washed in cold water;

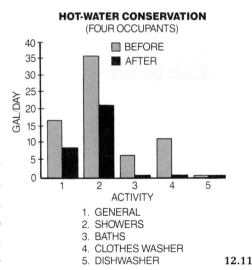

HOT-WATER CONSERVATION
(FOUR OCCUPANTS)

GAL/DAY

BEFORE
AFTER

ACTIVITY
1. GENERAL
2. SHOWERS
3. BATHS
4. CLOTHES WASHER
5. DISHWASHER

12.11

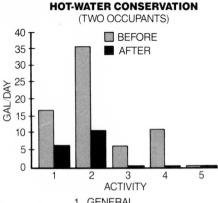

HOT-WATER CONSERVATION
(TWO OCCUPANTS)

GAL/DAY

☐ BEFORE
■ AFTER

ACTIVITY

1. GENERAL
2. SHOWERS
3. BATHS
4. CLOTHES WASHER
5. DISHWASHER

12.12

and we never did have an automatic dishwasher. Overall, daily consumption would drop from 70 gallons to 30 gallons — a 57 percent savings for the cost of a $15 showerhead and three $1.95 faucet aerators!

Illustration 12.12 shows the further drop in consumption that should result when our two teenaged sons leave home — an overall drop to 17 gallons per day, or a mere 24 percent of the present level.

SYSTEM RETROFIT

Somewhere on your present water heater (unless you, too, are heating water in a kettle!) is a thermostat; it is probably set at 140°. I don't know why manufacturers set thermostats at 140°. Perhaps, as with Detroit automakers, it is to impress us with superfluous power. In fact, most of us wash dishes and bathe at 100–110°, and we generally fiddle with the hot and cold controls for a wasteful minute or two before achieving a comfortable mix. My advice is to adjust your thermostat to its lowest setting, and then adjust it upward over time until you feel comfortable. Any temperature setting above 110–120° is wasteful unless you have an automatic dishwasher, and that can be rectified by pulling the plug! (Or, you can install a spot booster — see below.)

All of the other system retrofits we've previously discussed reduce standby losses. We should do the same with our hot-water system. First, it makes little sense to insulate your house with 4 to 12 inches of insulation and leave your hot-water heater clad in 1/2 inch! If sufficient clearance exists around your tank, install a "water heater insulation wrap," an item carried by all hardware stores for about $10.

While you're at the hardware store, pick up enough foam pipe insulation to cover the first 10 feet of hot-water pipe leading from the tank. (It's the pipe at the top that's giving off heat like a little radiator.)

There's not much we can do about the water stranded in the pipe after each use. Insulation slows, but doesn't stop, heat loss, and after several hours even the hot water in an insulated pipe will have lost most of its heat. We *can* prevent a little unproductive circulation of hot water, however! Remember "hot air rises"? Well, hot water rises too — straight up and out of the tank by convection within the hot water pipe itself. You can fool it and foil it by installing a "heat trap" — a 360° loop of pipe just above the tank, past which the hot water can't rise. Many new tanks contain heat traps. Some hardware stores carry retrofit traps for water heaters.

Altogether, the above retrofits should cut our standby losses by about half. Illustration 12.13 summarizes both conservation and system retrofit actions on the typical hot-water system.

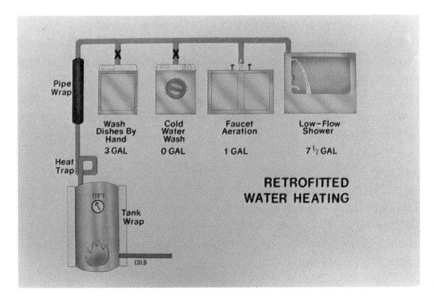

Pipe Wrap

Wash Dishes By Hand
3 GAL

Cold Water Wash
0 GAL

Faucet Aeration
1 GAL

Low-Flow Shower
7½ GAL

Heat Trap

Tank Wrap

RETROFITTED WATER HEATING

12.13

MAJOR SURGERY

Before tackling a system retrofit, you might consider major surgery — a total revamping of your hot-water system. My old electric tank was on its last legs, so major surgery was easy to contemplate. Even if you have a relatively new system, however, consider the alternatives below.

I performed a twenty-year life-cycle cost analysis of eight different water heating systems, including in the analysis the costs of installed equipment (and equipment replacement within twenty years, if likely), tank loss, pipe loss, and water-heating costs for the three levels of consumption: 70, 30, and 17 gallons per day. The eight systems are:

- *Electric resistance*. Estimated installed cost of $340; replacement after 10 years; efficiency 100 percent.
- *Electric heat pump*. Cost $965 plus tank replacement after 10 years; efficiency 200 percent.
- *Electric spot, or tankless*. Cost $455, plus $130 cost of tempering tank (see below); first 25° rise at cost of space heat due to tempering; efficiency 100 percent.
- *Oil separate*. Cost $745; replaced after 10 years; efficiency 70 percent.
- *Gas separate*. Cost $318; replaced after 10 years; efficiency 70 percent.
- *LP gas*. Cost $318; replaced after 10 years; efficiency 70 percent.
- *LP spot or tankless*. Cost $770; efficiency 70 percent.
- *Solar*. Cost $2,400 after 40 percent tax credit; 50 percent, 70 percent, and 75 percent solar fractions supplied for 70, 30, and 17 gallons per day.

All fuel costs per 100,000 Btu were those previously used in Chapter 2 for space heating.

Illustration 12.14 shows the results of the analysis: A, at my present consumption of 70 GPD; B, at a projected 30 GPD; and C, at a post-child 17 GPD.

The differences observed between graphs A, B, and C reflect a progressive shift of importance among three cost factors: (1) equipment cost, (2) standby loss, and (3) fuel price. The electric

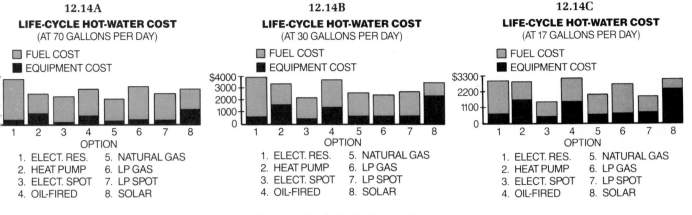

12.14A

LIFE-CYCLE HOT-WATER COST
(AT 70 GALLONS PER DAY)

☐ FUEL COST
■ EQUIPMENT COST

OPTION
1. ELECT. RES.   5. NATURAL GAS
2. HEAT PUMP   6. LP GAS
3. ELECT. SPOT 7. LP SPOT
4. OIL-FIRED   8. SOLAR

12.14B

LIFE-CYCLE HOT-WATER COST
(AT 30 GALLONS PER DAY)

☐ FUEL COST
■ EQUIPMENT COST

$4000
3000
2000
1000
0

OPTION
1. ELECT. RES.   5. NATURAL GAS
2. HEAT PUMP   6. LP GAS
3. ELECT. SPOT 7. LP SPOT
4. OIL-FIRED   8. SOLAR

12.14C

LIFE-CYCLE HOT-WATER COST
(AT 17 GALLONS PER DAY)

☐ FUEL COST
■ EQUIPMENT COST

$3300
2200
1100
0

OPTION
1. ELECT. RES.   5. NATURAL GAS
2. HEAT PUMP   6. LP GAS
3. ELECT. SPOT 7. LP SPOT
4. OIL-FIRED   8. SOLAR

heat pump and the solar system both have high initial cost but low effective fuel price, so that they compete well at high consumption levels. At the lowest consumption level of 17 GPD, the costs of equipment and standby loss become equal to fuel price in importance. For both of my future projected consumption levels of 30 and 17 GPD, the revolutionary electric spot or tankless heater promises to have the lowest total lifetime cost.

There are two types of spot water heater: gas and electric. I chose electric because natural gas is not available in my area and the LCC of an LP gas heater was greater than that of the electric version.

Electric spot heaters, if used as the sole source of hot water, require an adjustment of expectations. The model I installed is typical in that it draws about 40 amperes at 220 volts—about what a kitchen electric range would draw with all burners operating. (In case your eyebrows are quivering at this figure, the economy of the device lies in the fact that, although it consumes a tremendous current, it does so only while water is being drawn.) Even at that rate, however, the hot-water output is only 60 gallon-degrees per minute. In other words, we can draw 1 gallon per minute (GPM) raised 60°, or 2 GPM raised 30°, or 3 GPM raised 20°, etc.

We can draw water as slowly as necessary in washing dishes by hand, shaving, etc. But there is one use, critical to our conservation plan, which has a minimum acceptable flow. We have installed a low-flow showerhead in order to cut our bathing

LIFE WITH A SPOT WATER HEATER

water consumption by 50 percent. Experience shows that the lowest flow rate that will produce an acceptable spray from these devices is 1½ GPM.

At the rated output of the heater, the maximum temperature rise we can expect is therefore:

$$\frac{60 \text{ GPM}°}{1.5 \text{ GPM}} = 40°$$

Since normal showering temperature is 105°, water temperature at the heater input must be at least 105° − 40° = 65°, or room temperature. But, in the northern half of the United States, winter water temperatures are in the 35–45° range, so what are we to do?

The solution is "tempering," a trick employed long ago but now largely forgotten. It consists of letting incoming water reside in a tank within the heated space of the house long enough to warm to room temperature before entering the water heater. Tempering the incoming water (not all of the cold water, just that destined for the water heater) results in two benefits. First, the hot-water heater, operating over a smaller temperature rise, can produce hot water at a higher flow rate. Second, the initial 20–30° heating is accomplished at the space-heating rate per Btu in winter, and for free during the summer.

Tempering tanks are available through plumbing supply houses, and they are expensive. I constructed my own, which is both more effective and less expensive. I strapped 30 feet of 4″ schedule 40 PVC sewer pipe (stocked at most hardware and lumber stores) to my basement ceiling. Including all of the couplings and fittings, the material cost was $75. The capacity of my "tank" is 20 gallons. At my new hot-water consumption level of 30 GPD, the average droplet of water entering the spot heater has already resided in the tempering tank for two-thirds of a day—plenty of time for it to warm to 65°.

THE BOTTOM LINE

After both retrofitting my life-style and voluntarily submitting to the minor limitations of a spot water heater, what is the bottom-line savings? My annual hot-water bill should drop from a pre-retrofit $454 to a post-retrofit $81 — a reduction of 82 percent.

13. *Housewarming*

There are roughly 80,000,000 homes in the United States—25,000,000 of them, almost one-third, constructed more than forty years ago. Forty years is a significant length of time because that is the average period between major remodelings: additions, interior rearrangements, new kitchens, new bathrooms.

Remodeling is expensive; but it is usually justifiable. It turns an old house into a new house, and often at less cost than building from the ground up.

Energy efficiency has become one of the most important concerns of new homeowners. Home buyers and bank loan officers alike realize that total lifetime energy bills can equal or exceed the purchase price of a home.

I wrote this book for those 25,000,000 homeowners who, at one time or another, will consider remodeling. My aims were to demonstrate that:

- an older home can be remodeled to be just as energy-efficient as a new home;
- combining an energy retrofit with aesthetic remodeling is the most cost-efficient approach;
- energy savings alone will pay not only for the energy retrofit, but for the entire remodeling;
- in fact, you cannot afford not to retrofit!

Welcome to my housewarming. We began in Chapter 1 with a tour of the existing house and a view of some of my visions for a remodeled house. Follow me now and see how my dreams turned out.

We'll begin our tour outside, looking toward the south and east sides of the house (Illustration 13.1). The woodshed is gone, and in its place is a pleasant deck with space for my annual 3½ cords of firewood to dry in the sun. High on the south wall is my $360 master bedroom solar glazing. The old porch has been rebuilt (the right way, this time, with pressure-treated wood)

REMODELING

13.1

with a porch roof that, like a deciduous tree, sheds its awning every winter to admit sun to kitchen and dining area.

The north side is unchanged, except for a new pressure-treated porch deck. But the west side (Illustration 13.2) presents an entirely new facade. Gone are the ineffective and privacy-robbing half windows of the second floor. And in their place are three new skylights converting the upstairs to an exciting, well-lit space which, at night, will dump built-up heat. But best of all is the sunspace. Doubling the glazing area by installing floor-to-ceiling patio door panels proved to be a bit of solar alchemy. The sunspace literally converts the old house to a passive solar structure.

13.2

Let's go in through the kitchen (Illustration 13.3). Not much change here! Just an all-new kitchen designed for *serious* cooking. Unfinished (stained and finished by us) pine cabinets, and a well-broken-in 30″ × 72″ maple table top hold the cost to a minimum. Under the old linoleum, guess what we found—a maple floor!

13.3

Remember the old dining room with the bay window? Illustration 13.4 shows what we did with those old windows. The true effect can only be enjoyed, however, from the new

13.4

dining area across the room, Illustration 13.5. At ceiling level you can see the beam we installed back in Chapter 2 to replace the load-bearing wall which, unfortunately, separated the delightful spaces.

13.5

Turning to the right (Illustration 13.6), you can see the chimney we uncovered by removing the east-west wall (refer to Chapter 2). The wood stove behind the chimney now heats the entire house, with occasional help (much appreciated by the little old stove-stoker–coffee-maker — that's me) from the furnace in the basement and its master, a clock thermostat.

13.6

At the head of the lovely old staircase, now exposed, we find the bathroom (Illustration 13.7). As our energy auditor predicted, a little elbow grease proved that the old tub was as good as anything we could buy today. We also took her advice, and installed a water-saving showerhead and a new insulated water-saving toilet. I resisted the telephone man's suggestion to install a telephone in the bathroom (although he did convince me to wire the other rooms with outlets before drywalling all the walls), but I think time spent here will be much more pleasant under the new skylight.

13.7

All of the bedrooms received new gypsum drywall over walls and ceilings, as well as refurbished floors and windows, but when it came to the master bedroom (Illustration 13.8), we pulled out all the stops. Removing the low ceiling and installing the skylight made the room light and airy.

13.8

But removing the wall that enclosed the back stairway, chimney, and closet and installing two 34″ × 76″ patio door glazings made the room absolutely solar. I call it the Phoenix room. The clever bifolded trap door over the back stairway was the idea of a Maine boat-builder–carpenter, and lets us use the space next to the windows for reading.

While we were remodeling we kept energy uppermost in our minds. How well did we do in saving energy at the same time? Illustration 13.9 shows our annual energy costs before and after remodeling:

Heating	– $1,970 to $389, down 80 percent
Cooling	– $ 197 to $ 0, down 100 percent
Hot water	– $ 454 to $ 81, down 82 percent
Lights and appliances	– $ 408 to $306, down 25 percent

Overall, a drop from $3,029 to $776, or 75 percent. The figures speak for themselves.

Great! But was it worth it? Illustration 13.10 shows the cost versus lifetime savings of the retrofit measures in five categories. In estimating costs, I've listed the incremental retrofit costs — the extra costs of achieving energy savings over and above the costs of remodeling only.

Category	Cost	20-year saving
Insulation	$3,970	$22,120
Doors and windows	2,265	6,703
Hot water	475	7,476
Heating system	600	2,800
Passive solar	1,610	4,117
Totals	$8,920	$43,216

Most homeowners base energy conservation decisions on the *years to payback* — the number of years they have to wait to get the original investment returned in savings on their energy

ENERGY RETROFIT

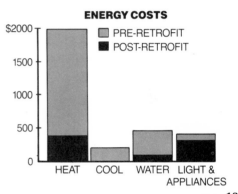

ENERGY COSTS
PRE-RETROFIT
POST-RETROFIT

HEAT   COOL   WATER   LIGHT & APPLIANCES

13.9

LIFETIME COST VS SAVINGS
OF RETROFIT CATEGORIES
SAVE
COST

1   2   3   4   5
CATEGORY
1. INSULATION
2. DOORS & WINDOWS
3. HOT WATER
4. WOOD STOVE
5. PASSIVE SOLAR

13.10

bills. I prefer *rate of return*. Financially, an investment in energy conservation is just one of a number of alternative investments I might make. For instance, I could speculate on land, put my money in a savings account, buy tax-free bonds, or install insulation. All of these investments annually return a dividend—a percentage of the investment above and beyond the principal of the investment itself—and do so indefinitely. In other words, energy conservation investments continue to pay an annual return even after they pay back.

The costs and savings of Illustration 13.10 translate into years to payback and tax-free annual rates of return of:

Category	Years to payback	Tax-free rate of return (percentages)
Insulation	3.6	28
Doors and windows	6.8	15
Hot water	1.3	77
Heating systems	4.3	23
Passive solar	7.8	13
Average	4.7	24

The cost of the combined retrofit and remodeling totaled approximately $25,000. This low figure was achieved because first, we worked *within* the existing building shell—never adding, only removing and refurbishing; second, in nearly every case we opted for the most cost-effective solution, rather than that which would impress.

The real estate agent who sold us the house established our first criterion—to invest only as much as would be returned upon sale as increased value. The neighborhood established a limit on ultimate value: $75,000. And before we started our project, the property was evaluated at $50,000. So our first goal was met; in a sense the remodeling has already paid back. From this point on, however, the annual saving of $2,160 represents an additional tax-free return on the investment of 8.6 percent.

Simply put—I couldn't afford not to.

Index

absorbing films, to block solar radiation, 119
acrylic inside storm windows, 105, 106
agricultural extension agent, 128
air: in insulation products, 135, 136, 137; material/air ratio and R value, 136, 137; R value of still, 135
air conditioner: life-cycle cooling cost, 127; sealing heat leaks around, 168
air conditioning, central: COP, 120; life-cycle cooling cost, 127
air exchange, 27; with furnace fan, 123; with whole-house fan, 122; with window fan, 120
air flow: cool, 41–44; cooling with natural, 124–127; warm, 33, 41–44
air gaps: in attic insulation, 138, 139–140; in problem areas, 140; at top of stud spaces, 149, 155. See also Heat leaks, hidden
air-gas mixture, in gas heating systems, 53
air infiltration, 118, 150, 151, 163. See also Heat loss
air leaks: through double-hung windows, 102; summer heat gain through, 118. See also Heat leaks, hidden
air-oil combustion balance, 51, 59
air temperature. See Temperature, air
air-to-air heat exchangers, 168
"Airtightness," 27, 117
Annual Fuel Utilization Efficiency (AFUE), 62
appliances: energy used for, 4; pre-retrofit and post-retrofit annual energy costs, 12, 197
Aquastat, 51; lowering temperature setting, 58–59; variable, 61
"Atmospheric burners," 53
Attic access panel. See Attic scuttle
Attic door, heat leaks around, 169. See also attic scuttle
Attic flat, insulating, 156–157; life-cycle costs, 157
Attic floor: air gaps in, 138–139; life-cycle costs of insulating, 140–141
Attic folding stairs, 86; air gaps in, 140; insulating, 90
Attic scuttle, 79, 169; how to build insulated, 90; insulating and weatherstripping options, 86–87; life-cycle cost of retrofitting, 87
audit. See Energy audit
Automatic vent damper, 60–61, 178
Awning, 70, 119, 120
Awning windows, 99

Backup heat: for solar water heater, 179; for wood stove, 46–47
Baling wire, 159
Balloon frame, 20, 21
Barometric damper, 50, 51; reducing heat loss in, 60, 166
Baseboard heating: electric resistance,

34, 35, 37, 38; with hot-water distribution systems, 54, 55
Baseboards, heat leaks around, 167
Basement, 11; air gaps in, 140; cooling with air from, 123, 124; heat leaks in, 166; insulating, 157–162; locating bearing walls in, 22; moisture in, 11; ventilating bathroom into, 168; windows, 99, 166
Basement bulkhead, 79; how to build insulated, 89; insulating and weatherstripping options, 86; life-cycle cost of retrofitting, 86; R value of, 86; sealing heat leaks, 166
Basement floor: cooling effect of, 123; heat loss through, 26; R value of, 146
Basement walls, 26, 147; cooling effect of, 123; heat loss through, 57, 153; insulating options, 147–148; insulating inside, 157, 159–160; insulating outside, 157, 160–162; life-cycle cost of retrofitting, 148
Bathing, 172
Bathroom, 10, 195; heating, 44; ventilating to basement, 168
Bathroom fan, 168
Bay window, 8, 9; converting to sunspace, 76, 192
Beadboard. See Polystyrene foam boards, molded
Beam, 21; replacing wall with, 23–24
Beans, pole, 119
Bearing wall, 21; identifying, 22; replacing, 23–24
Bedrooms, 10; master bedroom, 76, 189, 196, 197
Blanket and batt insulation. See Fiberglass batts; Fiberglass blankets
Blast tube, 34, 35, 49
Blower, oil-burner, 34, 35, 49, 52; standby losses in, 60. See also Furnace blower; Furnace fan
Blower door, 164
Blown-in insulation, 134, 136, 149, 156
Board, 19
Body: balancing temperature of, 113–116; comfort-zone chart, 114
Boiler modulating control, 61, 62
Boilers: dry-base, 50; gas, 53; oil-fired, 34, 35, 49, 50–51, 54–56; standby loss in, 61; steam, 50, 51; tankless water heaters with, 56, 59; wet-base, 50
Box sills, basement. See Sill
Braces, diagonal, 20–21
Breeze, 94, 100, 115
Btu (British thermal unit): cost of delivered heat per 100,000 Btu, 37; defined, 36, 180; in one gallon No. 2 fuel oil, 37
Building inspector, 24
Bulkhead door. See Basement bulkhead
Burglar-proofing doors, 84
Burner-off periods, 51, 57, 60

Cable entries, heat leaks around, 166, 167

Carbon dioxide, 32
Carbon monoxide, 32
"Carpenter Gothic," 6
Casement windows, 100
Cathedral ceiling, 146; options for insulating, 155–156; life-cycle costs, 156
Caulk: foam, 166; silicone, 109, 166
Caulking: cracks and joints, 27, 166; heat ducts, 170; holes, 166, 167; with passive solar heating, 69; to prevent summer heat gain, 117; around windows, 102, 109, 166
Ceiling, 193, 196
Ceiling fan: heat leaks around, 169; use with wood stove, 42
Ceilings, cathedral, 146, 155–156
Ceilings, sloping: insulating, 157; problems of blown-in insulation, 156; possibility of heat damage, 156
Cell structure of insulating materials, 135, 136, 137
Cellulose loose fill, 134; advantages and disadvantages, 136; composition of, 136; R value of, 134, 136
"Chimney effect," 50–51
Chimneys: cleaning out, 166; draft, 45; heat leaks around, 169; lining, 45; location in house, 40–41, 194; new installation of, 40; safety of, 44–45; suction in, 50–51
Circulator pumps, 35, 49, 50; in hot-water distribution system, 54, 55
Clearances: for stove, 40; for stove pipe, 46
Clock-driven override, 61
Clothes dryer: heat leaks around vent, 168; venting to furnace return duct, 168–169
Clothes drying, 168, 173
Clothes washing, hot water consumed in, 173, 181
Coal: cost per 100,000 Btu, 37; life-cycle heating cost, 38; and optimum R value of insulation, 141
Coefficient of Performance (COP): of air conditioners, 127; of central electric air conditioning, 120
Cole, John, 103
Combination storm-screen doors. See Doors
Combination windows. See Storm windows, outside
Combustion, 32, 33; achieving maximum efficiency, 50–51, 59; air-oil combustion balance, 51; in electric heating system, 34, 35; in gas heating systems, 53; in wood stoves, 33
Combustion chamber, 34, 35, 50
Combustion loss, 56–57, 60, 62
Comfort: defined, 113–114; and humidity and temperature, 114–116; level, 106; -zone chart, 114
Commercial energy use, 4
Compression, window motion, 107, 108
Concrete slab, solar energy storage in, 70

Condensation: how it occurs, 142–143; possibility of damage, 144; preventing under roof boards, 156; relationship to humidity and temperature, 144, 145; and vapor barrier, 144–145

Conduction: and energy flow, 113; and overheated house, 117, 118

Conservation, hot-water, 181–183

Conservation investment: costs and savings, 12–14, 197; criterion for amount of, 198; tax-free rate of return, 198; years to payback, 197, 198

Convection: and body heat, 115; cooling house through, 125; daytime solar heating by, 71; and energy flow, 113; of heat in water wall, 72; hot-water loss through, 183; and overheated house, 117, 118; reverse, 71

Convector pipes, 54, 55

Conversion: defined, 32; in electric heating system, 34, 35; in oil-fired boiler, 34, 35, 50; in wood stove, 33

Cooking, 174

Cooling: with basement air, 123–124; blocking solar radiation, 118–120; and comfort, 113–116; with electric heat pump, 179; home energy used for, 4, 12; life-cycle costs, 127; mechanical aids, 120–123; with movable window insulation, 104; by natural air flow, 124–127; passive, by pumping, 126–127; pre-retrofit and post-retrofit annual energy costs, 197; projected savings, 12; through windows, 94, 100

Costs, to achieve retrofit savings, 5, 11–14, 197–198. See also Life-cycle costs; specific entries

Cracks: in double-hung windows, 102, 107; heat loss through, 27; summer heat gain through, 118. See also Heat leaks, hidden

Creosote, 38, 46

Curing glue, 88, 110, 112

Damage, moisture, 144, 156

Dampers: automatic vent, 60–61, 178; barometric, 50, 51, 60, 166; fireplace, 169; in heat ducts, 54; plastic, 71; positive closure, 168

Defects, 27. See also Heat leaks, hidden

Degree days: defined, 48; and life-cycle costs of insulation, 140–141; and winter heat loss, 97

Dew point, 143, 144

Dining room, 2, 192, 193

Dishwasher, automatic, 181, 182

Dishwashing, 173, 182

Distribution medium, 34, 50, 51, 54

Diurnal swing, 67

Door frame, 84; air gaps around, 140, 166; fitting new doors to, 86, 88, 89

Doors: burglar-proofing, 84; combination storm-screen, 84; functions of, 80–83; how to build insulated, 87–90; life-cycle costs, 86, 87; lifetime cost versus retrofitting savings, 197; prehung, 84, 85; retrofitting options for, 85–86; sealing heat leaks in, 166; structure of, 83,

84; in thermal envelope, 26, 79–80; types, 7, 79, 85, 86; weatherstripping, 85, 88. See also Attic scuttle; Basement bulkhead

Doors, paneled: construction of, 83–84; R value of, 85

Dry-base boilers, 50

Drywall, gypsum: for attic scuttle, 87, 90; on bedroom walls, 196; thermal mass layer, 76, 127

Drywall joint compound, 166

Drywall joint tape, 161

Duct tape, 167, 170

Ducts, distribution, 34, 52, 54, 55; insulating, 54, 170

Duplex houses, "party" walls in, 170

Dust, in wall removal, 23–24

Efficiency, heating: Annual Fuel Utilization, 62; cost of delivered heat, 37; of electric heat pump, 37, 38, 179; of heating systems, 36–37; improving with equipment modifications, 60–62; improving with operating adjustments, 57–60; and life-cycle heating costs, 38; of water-heating systems, 56, 178–180, 184

Elbows, stove-pipe, 45

Electric cables: and bearing wall, 22; heat leaks around, 166

Electric heat pump: cooling with, 179; cost per 100,000 Btu, 37; efficiency of, 37, 38, 179; how it works, 179; lifecycle cost, 38; life-cycle costs of heating water by, 184, 185

Electric ignition for gas furnaces, 53, 61

Electricity, price rise of, 4

Electric radiant heater, 44

Electric receptacle, 149; heat leaks around, 150, 167

Electric resistance heating, 34, 35; cost per 100,000 Btu, 37; installation cost, 38; and optimum R value of insulation, 141; life-cycle cost, 38; water-heating system, life-cycle costs, 184, 185

Electric spot or tankless water heater: amperes drawn, 185; hot-water output per minute, 185; life-cycle costs, 184, 185; maximum temperature rise expected, 186; savings, 187; tempering tank for, 186

Electric hot water, 176, 177; hot-water output per hour, 176

Energy: price rise, 4; U.S. consumption, 3; use for heating water, 180–181; use in home, 4; use in pre-retrofit house, 12; use by sector, 4; where it goes, 56–57

Energy audit, 11–12, 15; oil need predicted by, 40

Energy costs, pre-retrofit and post-retrofit, 12, 197

Energy flows, and comfort, 113–116

Energy sources, 4

Entrance doors. See Doors

Equipment cost, and true cost, 37, 38

Equivalents: Btu, 36; masonry, 76

Excavating, for outside basement insulation, 160–161

Exterior walls, 116, 149–155; life-cycle costs of retrofitting options, 154–155; viewed through infrared scanner, 149–153

Evaporation: and energy flow, 113, 115; in insulated wall cavities, 144; by trees, 118

Fan limit switch, 52, 58, 59

Fan, oil-burner. See Blower, oil-burner

Fans: bathroom, 168; for summer cooling, 120–123

Faucet, outside, heat leaks around, 166

Faucet aerators, saving hot water with, 181

Fender washers, 161

Fiberglass, loose-fill, 134, 135; costs of insulating attic with, 140–141, 156–157; option for wall insulation, 154–155; R value, 136; for window pulley holes, 108, 155

Fiberglass batts, 134, 135; advantages and disadvantages, 135, 148; for heat leaks, 166, 169, 170; gaps in, on attic floor, 139–140; how to cut, 158; insulating basement walls with, 147, 148, 159; insulating between floor joists with, 158; R value, 27; standard widths, 139

Fiberglass blankets, 134, 135; advantages and disadvantages, 135; foil-faced, for basement wall, 159; unfaced, for cathedral ceiling, 155, 156

Filters, furnace, 59

Finance charges, 38

Firebox, wood-stove, 39, 40

Fire chamber, 33

Fire codes: for chimneys, 169; for egress, 103; for foam insulations, 86; for lighting fixtures, 169; for wood-stove hookups, 46

Fireplace damper, heat leaks in, 169

Fire-resistant insulation, 132, 134, 136

Fixed windows, 99; installing fixed double glazing, 108–109

Flame-retention-head oil burner, 60; savings with, 61, 62

Flashing, with basement insulation, 160, 161

Floor joists, 20; and bearing walls, 21, 22; insulating between, 135, 139–140, 158, 159

Flue gases, 32; buoyancy of, 50–51; energy loss in, 57; route of, 33, 34, 50

Flue pipe, 49, 50, 52, 53; barometric damper in, 50; standby losses up, 57, 180

Foam gaskets, 167

Floor registers: cooling with, 123, 124, 125; with wood stoves, 42, 44

Floors, 18, 20, 191

Foam insulation, blown-in, 134, 137

Foam insulation boards, 134, 136–137; cost of, 136; for insulated attic scuttle, 87, 90; for insulated bulkhead door, 86, 89; for insulating cathedral ceiling, 155–156; for insulated door, 88; for insulating walls, 148, 154–155, 160–162

Formaldehyde fumes, 137

Foundation, 20; insulating around, 161–162

Franklin, Benjamin, 33

Free-air rating, of whole-house fans, 122

From the Walls In (Wing), 24, 44

Fuel flow rate, reducing, 60

Fuel pump, 34

Fuel savings: with equipment modifications, 60–61; with operating modifications, 57–60; projected, 62

Furnace. *See* Oil furnace; Gas heating systems

Furnace blower, 54, 55; circulating clothes-dryer air with, 168–169. *See also* Blower, oil-burner; Furnace fan

Furnace fan, summer cooling with, 123–124, 127

Furnace filter, 52; access panel, 123; replacing, 59

Galvanized pipe, 45

Gas, liquid petroleum (LP): cost of heat per 100,000 Btu, 37; life-cycle heating cost, 38, 184; water heaters, 184, 185

Gas, natural: cost per 100,000 Btu, 37; life-cycle heating cost, 38; and optimum R value of insulation, 141; rise in price, 4

Gas heating systems, 53; ignition of, 53, 61; life-cycle costs, 38; servicing, 59; vent damper in, 61

Gas water heater, 178, 179; automatic vent dampers in, 178; life-cycle cost of, 184, 185; standby losses of, 178. *See also* Tankless water heaters

Glass: reflectivity of, 92, 95–96; transmission of light through, 95–96; transmission of heat through, 96–97

Glazing: for passive solar heating, 64, 69, 70–74; recommended ratio of glazing area to living area, 75; thermal storage mass for solar glazing, 74, 76. *See also* Triple glazing; Windows, double-glazed

"Glazing tape," 108, 109

Glue: carpenter's, 110, 112; epoxy, 88; Resorcinal, 88

Gothic Revival, 6

Greenhouse: average temperature and relative humidity, 144; and passive solar heat, 65, 67, 73

Gypsum drywall. *See* Drywall, gypsum

Hall, front, 9, 10

Hardware, door: saving, 87

Heat: backup, 46–47, 179; buildup, 156; escape, 26; net winter heat gain, 97–99, 118; radiation, 33, 113; removal, 123; storage, 69–73, 74, 76; summer heat gain, 117–129, 131; transmitted through glass, 96–97; trap, 183; useful, 57, 62

Heat costs: annual costs, pre-retrofit and post-retrofit, 197; life-cycle costs, 38; per 100,000 Btu, 37; pre-retrofit and post-retrofit costs, 12; relative and true costs, 36–38

Heat distribution, 32, 33; efficiency, 36; of electric heating system, 34, 35; in hot-water heating system, 54, 55;

losses through, 57; medium for, 34, 50, 51; in warm-air system, 54, 55; and wood stove, 41, 44; zoned, 54

Heat exchanger, 34; air-to-air, for bathroom fan, 168; cleaning, 59; heat loss through, 51, 56, 57; and hot-water distribution system, 54; of oil furnace, 50, 51, 52; of oil hot-water heater, 177; of tankless water heater, 56; of warm-air distribution system, 54; waste in burner-off periods, 57

Heat flow, 24, 25; and R values in air cavities, 138; around and through thermal envelope, 26, 27, 117, 124–126; from wood stove, 33

Heating: energy used for, 4; pre-retrofit energy use, 12

Heating systems: efficiency, 36–37, 62; electric resistance baseboards, 34; electric heat pumps, 38; functions of, 28–31; furnaces and boilers, 48–56; how they work, 32–35; lifetime costs versus savings of retrofit categories, 197; modifications to improve efficiency, 60–62; operating adjustments to improve efficiency, 57–60; true-cost–life-cycle cost, 37–38; wood stoves, 38–40; years to payback and tax-free rate of return, 198

Heat leaks, hidden, 163–165; in attic areas, 169–170; in basement areas, 166; in living areas, 150, 166–169

Heat loss, 26, 27, 163; through basement, 26, 57, 153, 158, 159, 160; body, 114, 115; around doors, 80; from heat exchanger, 51, 56, 57; reducing in gas system, 61; and solar heating, 67, 68; from water heater, 152; around windows, 97–98. *See also* Air gaps; Heat leaks, hidden

Hinges, "loose pin," 112

Hopper window, 99

Hot water: average American consumption per day, 181; energy costs before and after retrofitting, 12, 197; energy used for, 4, 180–181; four-person daily consumption, 181; loss, 4, 183; savings through conservation, 181–182; savings through system retrofit, 182–183; savings through system revamping, 184–187; two-person daily consumption, 182; uses of, 171–174; years to payback and tax-free rate of return, 198. *See also* Water heating and distribution system

Hot-water boiler, 34, 35; distribution system of, 54, 55; with tankless water heater, 51, 56, 59, 61, 178–179

Hot-water heaters, 54; types, 56, 175–180

House: frame, 20–21; functions of, 15–18, 24–25; heat gain in, 117–118; model, 9; plan, 6–11, 77; structure of, 19–22; temperature and relative humidity of average, 144; volume of, 122; weight of, 19. *See also* Thermal envelope

"House doctors," 164

Household furnishings, in thermal mass, 76

Humidity, relative: and comfort level,

114–116; and condensation, 143–145; defined, 142

Hydronic boiler, 34, 35; distribution system of, 54, 55

Hygrometer, 145

Ice-dams, 156

Ignition, electric, 53, 61

Incident angle of solar radiation, 95

Industrial energy use, 4

Infiltration, air, 150, 151, 163; summer heat gain through, 118. *See also* Air leaks; Heat loss

Inflation, 38

Infrared radiation, 33

Infrared scanner: finding air gaps with, 149, 164; tour of house, 150–153

Inspection of wood-stove hookups, 46

Insulated doors: buying, 85; building, 86; how to build, 87–90

Insulating: attic ceiling and flat, 140–141, 156–157; basements, 86, 147–149, 157–162; cathedral ceiling, 155–156; distribution pipes, 54; doors, 86–90; exterior walls, 149–155; foundation, 161–162; hidden heat leaks, 166–170; with passive solar heating, 69; around window frame, 155; windows, 72, 73–74, 104–107

Insulation: as conservation investment, 13; figuring optimum level, 140–141, 157; functions of, 130–133; increasing R value through, 27; lifetime cost versus savings of retrofitting, 197; material/air ratio, 135, 136, 137; problem areas, 140; properties of, 134; sloppy installation, 138, 139–140; types of, 134, 135–137; years to payback and tax-free rate of return, 198

Insulation, fiberglass. *See* Fiberglass *entries*

Insulation, foam. *See* Foam insulation *entries*

Insulation, movable window. *See* Movable window insulation

Insurance company, and smoke detectors, 46

Interior spaces, altering, 22–24

Interior walls, heat leaks in, 170

Jacket losses, 57; in hot-water tanks, 180

Joints: heat loss through, 27, 102; securing stove pipe, 45–46

Joists, floor, 20; and bearing walls, 21, 22; insulating between, 135, 139–140, 157–159

Kerosene: cost per 100,000 Btu, 37; life-cycle cost, 38

Keyholes, filling, 166

Kitchen, 9, 191; entrance doors, 79

Knee-wall drawers, insulating, 167–168

Knobs, 112

Lath: removing, 23; saving, 24

Law of Diminishing Returns: and attic insulation, 157; and insulation thickness, 140; and window layers, 97–99

LCC. *See* Life-cycle costs
Life-cycle costs: of cooling, 127; of delivered heat, 37; of heating, 38; of retrofitting attic, 87, 140–141, 157; of retrofitting basement, 86, 148; of retrofitting cathedral ceiling, 156; of retrofitting doors, 86, 87; of retrofitting single-glazed windows, 103; of retrofitting walls, 154–155; of water-heating systems, 184–185; of window retrofitting options, 106
Lifetime cost versus savings, of retrofit categories, 197
Light, and windows, 93, 95–96
Lighting, energy used for, 4, 197
Lighting fixtures, recessed: air gaps around, 140; heat leaks around, 169
Living areas, heat leaks in, 166–169
Living room, 9, 194
Load-bearing functions, of house components, 20–22. *See also* Bearing wall
Lofts, heating of, 42, 43
Long-fiber fiberglass insulation, 134, 135, 136
Loose-fill insulation, 134, 136, 140, 157
LP gas. *See* Gas, liquid petroleum (LP)

Magnets, 105
Mail slot, sealing, 166
Maintenance, 37, 38, 59, 67, 177
Maple trees, 118, 128
Masonry walls: insulating, 161–162; and drywalls, 76; and household furnishings, 76; rule of thumb for thermal mass, 74, 76; use in solar heating, 69, 70, 71, 72
Mason's twine, 159
Mastic, building, 90
Material/air ratio, in R value of insulation, 135, 136, 137
Medicine cabinet, heat leaks around, 167
Meeting rails, of double-hung windows, 101, 102, 107
Moisture: in basements, 11; damage, 144, 156; preventing under roof boards, 156; sources of household, 145; and vapor barriers, 142–145
Moisture-resistant insulation, 132, 134, 136, 137
Mother Earth News, The, 67
Movable window insulation (MWI): cooling with, 104; and comfort level, 106, 107; life-cycle costs of, 106; at night, 72, 73–74; 104–106
Mylar: inside storm window, 104; dampers, 71

Nail gun, 161
Nails: aluminum, 161; galvanized, 161; roofing, 89, 158
Natural cooling, 124–127. *See also* Cooling; Pumping
Newsprint, shredded, 136
Nitrogen dioxide, 32
Noncombustible floor covering, for wood stove, 46
Noncombustible insulation, 134, 136
Noncombustible shield for stove, 46

Nozzle, oil furnace, 35, 49, 50; reducing size, 60

Oak trees, 118
Off-time, furnace, minimizing, 60
Oil, fuel: Btu in one gallon of No. 2 fuel oil, 37; cost per 100,000 Btu, 37; life-cycle heating cost, 38; and optimum R value of insulation, 141; percentage of maximum useful heat from, 57; price rise of, 4
Oil burner, flame-retention-head, 60
Oil-fired boiler, 34, 35; how it works, 49, 50–51; with tankless water-heating coil, 51, 52, 56, 61
Oil furnace, 51, 52; as backup system, 47; differences from oil boiler, 51; ducts, 54, 55; energy waste, 57; maintenance, 59; reducing nozzle size, 60; retention-head-burner, 61
Oil water heater, 177–178; hot-water output per hour, 177; life-cycle costs of, 184, 185; standby loss, 178; tankless, 56, 178–179
On-time, furnace, maximizing, 60
Optimum level of insulation (optimum R), 140–141, 157
Overhangs, roof, 17, 70, 156
Overheating, 117–118; with passive solar heat, 69–70; of roof boards, 156

Parlor, 9
"Party" walls, heat leaks in, 170
Passive Solar Design Handbook (DOE), 74, 77
Passive solar heat: defined, 63–64; expectations of, 64–67; lifetime costs versus savings, 197; from masonry wall, 70–71; modifications for house, 76–78; performance, 73–74, 77–78; ratio of glazing area to living area, 75; from south-facing windows, 69–70; from sunspace, 72–73; target performance, 75; thermal storage mass for, 74, 76; from water wall, 71–72; years to payback and tax-free rate of return, 198
Patio door, 100; for fixed double-glazed windows, 108–109; in master bedroom, 76, 189, 196, 197
Perlite loose-fill insulation, 134, 136
Pilot light, gas heating system, 53, 61
Pine molding, for strapping, 110
Pipe: blue-steel, 45; galvanized, 45
Pipes: convector, 54, 55; distribution, 34, 35, 54; flue, 50, 53, 177; stove, 45–46; water, 180, 182
Plank. *See* Board
Plaster, removing, 23–24
Plastic film: for additional glazing, 104, 106; for increased sunlight transmission, 95–96. *See also* Mylar
Plumbing stack vent, heat leaks around, 165, 170
Plywood: CDX, 89; dam for attic scuttle, 90; Lauan, 87, 88
Pollutants, 32
Polyethylene sheeting: for insulating be-

tween floor joists, 158; as vapor barrier, 145
Polyisocyanurate foam insulation, 134, 137
Polystyrene, extruded, 134, 137; applying to basement wall, 160–161
Polystyrene foam boards, molded, 134, 136–137
Polyurethane foam insulation, 134, 137
Porch, 6–7, 189; deck, 190; roof, 76, 190
Positive closure fan dampers, 168
Post, 20, 21, 23
Pressurization technique for finding heat leaks, 164–165
Pressurizing blower, of gas furnace, 53
Privacy, 92
Properties of home insulations, 134
Pulley holes, 102; insulating, 108, 155, 166–167
Pumping, of cool air, 126–127
Pumps, circulator. *See* Circulator pumps
Putty, 166–167
Putty knife, 163, 167
PVC sewer pipe, 186

Radiation. *See* Heat; Solar radiation
Radiators, 54
Rafter, 19, 20, 21; insulating, 135, 156
Rails, window, 101, 102; air leaks through, 102; meeting, 101, 102, 107; motion between window frame and, 107
Range hood, heat leaks around, 165, 168
Rate of return (tax-free) on conservation investment, 198
Reflective film to block solar radiation, 119
Reflectivity of glass, 92; decreasing, 95–96
Registers: floor, 42, 44, 123–124; warm-air outlet and return, 54, 123–124
Relative humidity. *See* Humidity, relative
Remodeling: combined retrofitting and, 12, 198; house after, 189–196; house before, 6–11; period between major remodelings, 12, 188; reasons for, 188
Residential energy use, 4
Resorcinal, 88
Retrofitting, 5–6, 11; combined with remodeling, 12, 198; costs to achieve savings, 5, 13–14; cumulative effect of heating-system, 62; doors, 85–87; lifetime cost versus savings, 197; maximum useful heat achieved with, 57; water-heating system, 182–183
Rock-wool insulation, 134; blankets and batts, 134, 136; blown-in, 149, 156; loose-fill, 134, 136; settling of, 149, 151, 154
Roof boards, 21; moisture under, 156; overheating, 156
Roof overhang, 17, 70, 176
Roofs, 21, 25; snow on, 17, 19, 20; in thermal envelope, 26
Root ball: of shrubs, 160; of tree, 128, 129
Rule of thumb for thermal mass, 70, 74–76

R value, 27; of acrylic panels, 105; air activity in air cavities, 138; attic insulation, 138, 139, 140, 157; basement bulkhead, 86; basement floor, 146; basement wall, 148; defined, 27; double-glazed windows, 97; exterior wall, 149; guide to optimum ceiling/wall R values, 141; of home insulation materials, 27, 134, 136, 137; "manufactured," and "aged," 137; of paneled door, 85; and rate of temperature drop, 143; of repaired entrance doors, 86; of single-glazed window, 27, 96; of still air, 135, 138; of stone, 96; of triple-glazed windows, 140

Safety, and wood stove, 44–46. See also Fire codes
Sash, window, 101, 107; keeping up, 102; motion between frame and, 107; removing, 108
Sash weights, 102; air leaks through pulley holes, 102; removing, 108
Saturation curve, 142–143
Savings: on annual hot-water bill, 187; annual on retrofitted, remodeled house, 198; cost versus lifetime, of retrofitting, 197; costs to achieve retrofit, 4, 5; energy, 12–14; heating, with five-degree setback, 58; incremental, of multiple window layers, 97; with movable window insulation, 106; with passive solar heat, 74–78; projected, with retrofitted heating system, 62
Scissors, 163
Screen doors, 82
Screen molding, in insulated door, 88
Screwdriver, power, 88
Screws: brass roundhead, 109; drywall, 88
Sears, Roebuck and Company, 81
Setting blocks, neoprene rubber, 108–109
Shade, roll-down, 105–106
Sheetrocked walls, double-, 70
Shingles, shimming with, 23, 24
Short-fiber fiberglass insulation, 134, 136, 155, 157
Showerheads, 172; water-saving, 181, 182, 185, 195
Showering, and hot-water output, 172, 181
Shrinking of wood, 83, 84
Shrubs, 148, 160, 162
Shutters, interior, 105, 106; and cooling, 119, 120; how to build insulating, 109–112
Silicone caulk, 109, 166; and paint, 109
Sill, 20, 21; air gaps around basement, 140; insulating, 159, 166
Ski chalets, 42, 43
Skylights: in bathroom, 195; in bedrooms, 190, 196; and summer cooling, 124, 125, 126
Sleeping, arrangements for, 121
Sliding tracks, 105
Sliding window, 100
Smoke detectors, 46
Smoke pencil, 164

Snow, weight of, 19, 20
Social value of stove location, 40, 41
Soffit, 156
Soil, and insulating of basement, 161, 162
Solar balance: with window insulation, 74; winter window, 73
Solar clothes dryer, 168
Solar collectors: masonry wall, 70–71; south-facing windows, 69–70; for solar water heaters, 179–180; sunspace, 72–73; water wall, 71–72. See also Thermal mass
Solar energy, 63–64; flows of, 77. See Passive solar heating; Solar collectors; Thermal mass
Solar gain, 67, 69, 70–72; of double- and triple-glazed windows, 98–99; in summer, 70, 117, 118; and winter heat gain, 97; winter window, 73
Solar greenhouse, 67, 73
Solar heat: active, 63–64, 95; passive, see Passive solar heat
Solar radiation, 70, 71; conversion to heat, 70, 71, 72; maximum, 73–74; percentage transmitted through glass, 95, 97–98; and summer heat gain, 104, 117, 118–120; and winter heat gain, 118
Solar savings (SSF), rule of thumb for thermal mass, 74, 76
Solar water heaters, 179–180; electric backup element for, 179; life-cycle cost of, 184, 185; percentage of hot water provided by, 180; typical installed cost, 180
Soleplate, heat leaks around, 167
Soot buildup, 59
Spade, backward, 128
Split-level house, placing stove in, 42, 43
Spot or tankless water heaters, 179; electric, 184, 185, 186; gas, 179, 184; hot-water output per minute, 185; life-cycle cost of, 184, 185; tempering water for, 186. See also Tankless water heaters
Stack gases, 32
Stack losses, 57; reducing, 60
Stairway, back, 10, 195
Standby losses, 57, 62; in boiler, 59, 61, 62; in furnace, 58–59, 60; of hot-water heaters, 178, 179, 180, 182–183; percentage of typical hot-water bill, 180
Staple gun, 163
Staples, carpentry, 110
Steam boilers, 50, 51
Steam pressure switch, 51
Stone, R value of, 96
Storage, solar heat, 69–73, 74, 76
Storm doors, 83, 84, 86; disadvantages of, 84
Storm windows, inside: acrylic, 105, 106; for basement, 166; glass, 105, 106; life-cycle costs, 106; Mylar, 104
Storm windows, outside, life-cycle costs, 103
Stove pipe, 45–46
Strapping: for insulating shutters, 110; for insulating basement walls, 159, 160

Stud, 19, 20, 21; air gaps at top, 140, 149; air leaks through spaces, 102; insulation for, 135
Stud wall: building in basement, 148; constructing temporary, 23; removing, 24; water containers in, 72
Suction in chimney, 50–51
Sulfur dioxide, 32
Summer heat gain, 117–129, 131. See also Cooling
Summer solar interventions, 70, 118–120
Sunscreens, 119
Sunspace: converted from bay window, 76, 77; creating for passive solar heat, 65, 72; in remodeled house, 190; sharing heat from, 72–73
Swelling of wood, 83, 84
Switch cover plates, 149

Tankless water heaters (with boilers), 51, 52; and clock-driven override, 61; efficiency of, 56, 178–179; lowering aquastat setting, 59
Tankless water heaters (without boilers): electric, 179, 184–186; gas, 179, 185
Target passive solar heating performance, 75
Tax credits, federal: for window retrofitting, 106; for solar water heaters, 184
Tax-free return on conservation investment, 198
Taxes, 37
Telephone cable, heat leaks around, 166
Telephone outlets, 195
Television antenna, caulking cable holes, 167
Temperature, air: and comfort level, 114–116; and condensation, 143–145; and relative humidity, 142–143
Temperature, body, 113; and comfort level, 114–116
Temperatures: average difference between indoor and outdoor, 57; of average house, 144; U.S. average daily highs and lows during August, 126, 127
Temperature swings, indoor, 69; before and after retrofitting, 125, 126; moderating with outside insulation, 160
Tempering tank, 186
Termites, poisoning, 161
Thermal envelope, 25–26, 79; and basement, 158, 159, 160; and heat escape and flow, 26–27; of retrofitted house, 146–147; and R value, 27; summer heat gains through, 117; ventilating for summer cooling, 124; wrapping with polyethylene, 145
Thermal mass, 67, 69, 70; drywall as, 76, 127; equivalents, 76; masonry wall, 70–71; and natural cooling, 123, 127; rule of thumb for ratio to glazing area, 70, 74, 75, 76; sunspace, 72; water wall, 71–72
Thermal resistance. See R value
Thermoply, 110, 112

Thermostat: boiler, 23, 51, 53; clock, 47, 58; furnace, 51–52, 53; hot-water heater, 182; setback, 57–58; wall, 51. *See also* Aquastat

Timer switch, 44

Toilet, water-saving, 195

Transportation energy use, 4

Trapdoor, bifolded, 197. *See also* Attic scuttle

Trees, deciduous: how to move, 128, 129; protecting, 129; for summer shading, 70, 118, 119; water evaporation by, 118

Triple glazing; net heat gains, 98, 99; R value of, 140; solar radiation transmitted through, 95

Trombé wall, 70

Tune-up, oil-burner, 59

Two-story house, placing stove in, 42, 43

United States energy consumption, 3, 4

Urea formaldehyde, 134, 137

Vacuuming furnace filters, 59

Vapor barrier, 142–145; below attic, 157, 158; extruded polystyrene boards, 137; function of, 145; for heat leaks, 167–168; in insulated basement, 158, 159, 160; and moisture damage, 156; polyethylene sheeting, 145

Velcro strips for sealing shades, 105

Vent damper. *See* Automatic vent damper

Ventilation: through doors, 82; through natural convection, 125–127; through windows, 82, 94, 99. *See also* Air flow

Venting: bathroom into basement, 168; between insulation and roof boards, 156; dryer outlet to furnace return duct, 168–169; masonry wall areas, 71

Vents, heat leaks around: clothes-dryer, 168; plumbing stack, 170

Vermiculite loose-fill insulation, 134, 136

Vines, to block solar radiation, 119

Volume: of house, 122; of wood-stove firebox, 39–40

Wall, bearing. *See* Bearing wall

Wall cavities: evaporation and condensation in, 143–144; insulation for, 136, 137; temperature drop in, 143; and vapor barrier, 144–145

Wall receptacles. *See* Electric receptacle

Wall studs. *See* Stud

Walls, exterior. *See* Exterior walls

Walls, interior. *See* Interior walls

Wall switches, insulating behind, 167

Warm-air distribution system, 54, 55

Washing-shaving, hot water consumed by, 174

Waste: of energy, 3, 56–57; of gas, 53, 61; of hot water, 171

Water: medium for heat distribution, 50; physical states of, 142; pounds recommended for water wall, 74. *See also* Hot water

Water heater insulation wrap, 182

Water-heating coil, tankless, 35, 51. *See also* Tankless water heaters (with boilers)

Water heating and distribution system, 175; heat loss from, 152; installing new system, 184–185; insulating tank, 182; insulating hot-water pipe, 182; life-cycle costs, 184–185; retrofitting, 182–183; types of, 175–180

Water-resistant insulation, 132, 134, 136, 137, 155

Water-saving toilet, 195

Water vapor, 32, 142–143; and vapor barriers, 144–145

Water wall for passive solar heating, 71–72

Weatherstrip: compressible self-adhesive foam, 108, 112; plastic-tension strip, 88, 89, 108

Weatherstripping: attic scuttle, 86, 90; bulkhead, 86, 89; doors, 85, 88; double-hung window, 102, 107–108; insulating shutters, 112; movable joints, 27; and passive solar heating, 69; to prevent summer heat gain, 117

Weight of house, 19–22

Wet-base boilers, 50

Whole-house fan, 122, 123

Window fan, 120–121

Window frame, 101, 102; air gaps around, 140; insulating around, 155; motion between window sashes and, 107

Windows: basement, 99, 166; cooling through, 94, 100; cost-effectiveness of multiple layers, 97; functions of, 91–94; heat leaks around, 166–167; heat loss around, 97–98; heat transmitted through, 96–97; lifetime cost versus savings of retrofitting, 197; light and, 93, 95–96; movable window insulation, 72, 73–74, 104–107; and passive solar heating, 64; replacing existing, 108; solar radiation transmitted through, 95, 117, 118; in thermal envelope, 25, 26; types, 99, 100; winter solar gain through, 73–74, 97–99; years to payback and tax-free rate of return, 198

Windows, combination. *See* Storm windows

Windows, double-glazed: installing fixed double-glazing, 103, 108–109; life-cycle costs, 106; retrofitting options for, 104–106; R value of, 97; solar gain from, 97–98; solar radiation transmitted through, 95

Windows, double-hung, 100, 101, 102; air leaks through, 102; caulking, 102; replacing, 103, 108–109; weatherstripping, 102, 107–108

Windows, single-glazed: air infiltration around, 151; life-cycle cost of retrofitting options, 103; R value of, 95; solar gain and heat loss from, 97–98; transmission of light through, 95

Windows, south-facing: direct-heat gain through, 69–70; net gain of triple glazing, 98–99; net heat gain of, 98; solar balance with insulation, 74; thermal storage and, 74, 76; winter solar gain and balance, 73

Window sash. *See* Sash, window

Windowshades, 119, 120

Window stops, 109, 112

Winter heat gain, and windows, 73–74, 97–99, 118

Winter heat loss: and windows, 97–98; and movable window insulation, 104, 106. *See also* Heat loss

Wiping, window motion, 107, 108; weatherstrip for, 108

Wood (fuel): cost per 100,000 Btu, 37; daily consumption of, 39; life-cycle heating cost, 38; and optimum R value of insulation, 141; projected cost of five cords, 63

Wood: components of house, 20–21; pressure-treated, 189; seasonal swelling and shrinking, 83, 84; strength of, 19, 2

Woodshed, 7, 8–9, 10, 189

Wood stove, 33; and air flow, 41–43; backup system for, 46–47; clearances for, 46; dirtiness of, 30; inspecting, 46; locations for, 40, 41, 42, 44; in remodeled house, 194; and safety, 44–46; selecting, 38; sizing, 39–40; stoking, 38–39

Years to payback on conservation investment, 197–198

Zoned heat, 54